Adobe® Photoshop® Elements 7

Kate Binder

que®

Contents

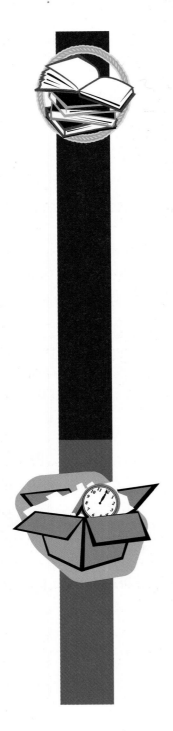

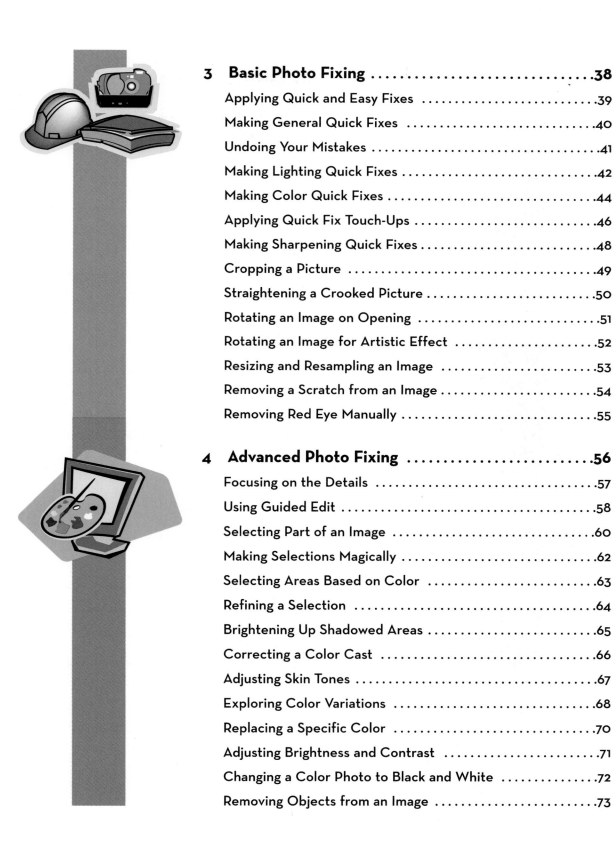

EASY ADOBE® PHOTOSHOP® ELEMENTS 7

ISBN-13: 978-0-7897-3926-1
ISBN-10: 0-7897-3926-7

Library of Congress Cataloging-in-Publication Data:

Binder, Kate.

Easy Adobe Photoshop elements 7 / Kate Binder.

p. cm.

Includes index.

ISBN-13: 978-0-7897-3926-1

ISBN-10: 0-7897-3926-7

1. Adobe Photoshop elements. 2. Photography—Digital techniques. 3. Image processing—Digital techniques. I. Title.

TR267.5.A33B562 2009

775—dc22

2008046113

Printed in the United States of America

First Printing: December 2008

U.K. ISBN-13: 978-0-7897-3927-8

U.K. ISBN-10: 0-7897-3927-5

First Printing: December 2008

TRADEMARKS

WARNING AND DISCLAIMER

BULK SALES

Que Publishing offers excellent discounts on this book when ordered in quantity for bulk purchases or special sales. For more information, please contact

U.S. Corporate and Government Sales

1-800-382-3419

corpsales@pearsontechgroup.com

For sales outside the United States, please contact

International Sales

international@pearson.com

Associate Publisher
Greg Wiegand

Acquisition and Development Editor
Laura Norman

Managing Editor
Patrick Kanouse

Senior Project Editor
Tonya Simpson

Copy Editor
Keith Cline

Indexer
Tim Wright

Proofreader
Kathy Ruiz

Technical Editor
Lisa Sihvonen-Binder

Publishing Coordinator
Cindy J. Teeters

Book Designer
Ann Jones

Compositor
Bronkella Publishing LLC

ABOUT THE AUTHOR

Kate Binder has mastered Photoshop and several other graphics programs over the past 20 years and is starting to feel quite old. She still enjoys tinkering with photos and does so at every opportunity. (It's much more entertaining than doing actual work.) When she can be found working, Kate is most likely to be doing magazine or book production, creating ebooks for major publishers, or writing books like this one. Books Kate has written or cowritten include *Sams Teach Yourself Adobe Photoshop Elements 6 in 24 Hours* (Sams, 2008), *The iMac Portable Genius* (Wiley, 2008), *Easy Mac OS X Leopard* (Que, 2007), *Sams Teach Yourself Adobe Photoshop CS4 in 24 Hours* (Sams, 2008), *Easy Adobe Photoshop Elements 4* (Que, 2005). Kate lives in an old house in New Hampshire with her husband, journalist Don Fluckinger, and assorted children, greyhounds, cats, and (she's pretty sure) a mouse under the dryer.

Kate's Website is http://www.prospecthillpub.com.

DEDICATION

To Allison. You're rockin' it, girl.

ACKNOWLEDGMENTS

My thanks go first to my family, as always: my husband and partner, Don, who makes me lunch every day; our kids, Patrick and Pinkie, who amaze me every day; and my parents, Richard and Barbara, without whom... well, that's pretty obvious. And thank you once more to Laura Norman at Que, for walking me through another one. The rest of the gang at Que deserves kudos, too, especially project editor Tonya Simpson, copy editor Keith Cline, and technical editor Lisa Sihvonen-Binder.

Many of the models for the photos in this book are retired racing greyhounds—a most extraordinary breed of dog. To learn more about how greyhounds make wonderful pets, visit http://www.adopt-a-greyhound.org.

WE WANT TO HEAR FROM YOU!

As the reader of this book, *you* are our most important critic and commentator. We value your opinion and want to know what we're doing right, what we could do better, what areas you'd like to see us publish in, and any other words of wisdom you're willing to pass our way.

As an associate publisher for Que Publishing, I welcome your comments. You can email or write me directly to let me know what you did or didn't like about this book—as well as what we can do to make our books better.

Please note that I cannot help you with technical problems related to the topic of this book. We do have a User Services group, however, where I will forward specific technical questions related to the book.

When you write, please be sure to include this book's title and author as well as your name, email address, and phone number. I will carefully review your comments and share them with the author and editors who worked on the book.

Email: feedback@quepublishing.com

Mail: Greg Wiegand
          Associate Publisher
          Que Publishing
          800 East 96th Street
          Indianapolis, IN 46240 USA

READER SERVICES

Visit our website and register this book at informit.com/register for convenient access to any updates, downloads, or errata that might be available for this book.

IT'S AS EASY AS 1-2-3

Each part of this book is made up of a series of short, instructional lessons, designed to help you understand basic information.

1 Each step is fully illustrated to show you how it looks onscreen.

2 Each task includes a series of quick, easy steps designed to guide you through the procedure.

3 Items that you select or click in menus, dialog boxes, tabs, and windows are shown in **bold**.

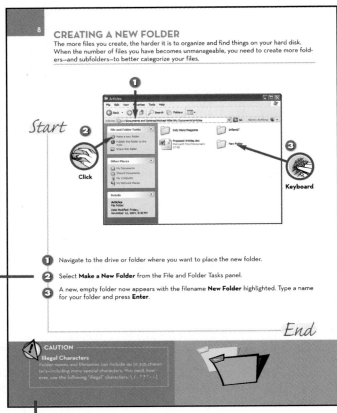

CREATING A NEW FOLDER

The more files you create, the harder it is to organize and find things on your hard disk. When the number of files you have becomes unmanageable, you need to create more folders—and subfolders—to better categorize your files.

1 Navigate to the drive or folder where you want to place the new folder.

2 Select **Make a New Folder** from the File and Folder Tasks panel.

3 A new, empty folder now appears with the filename **New Folder** highlighted. Type a name for your folder and press **Enter**.

CAUTION

Illegal Characters
Folder names and filenames can include up to 255 characters—including many special characters. You can't, however, use the following "illegal" characters: \ / : * ? " < > |

How to Drag:
Point to the starting place or object. Hold down the mouse button (right or left per instructions), move the mouse to the new location, then release the button.

Drag

Click

Tips, notes, and cautions give you a heads-up for any extra information you may need while working through the task.

Click:
Click the left mouse button once.

Keyboard

Click & Type:
Click once where indicated and begin typing to enter your text or data.

Selection:
Highlights the area onscreen discussed in the step or task.

Double-click:
Click the left mouse button twice in rapid succession.

Right-click:
Click the right mouse button once.

Pointer Arrow:
Highlights an item on the screen you need to point to or focus on in the step or task.

INTRODUCTION

I love Photoshop Elements, I really do.

Now, that's a statement that might surprise people who know me—in other words, people who know that I make a lot of my living working with "Big Photoshop" and its professional-level siblings in Adobe's powerful Creative Suite. Nonetheless, Photoshop Elements has a special place in my heart. And I'm sure you'll feel the same way by the time you've finished reading this book.

Look at it this way. You've got a digital camera (and probably a scanner, too). You've got this desktop PC that's hundreds—no, thousands—of times more powerful than the computers of just a few decades ago. Maybe you even have a cell phone that can take photos. How about your PDA? I bet it can do the same.

You've got all the gadgets. But let's face it; one thing you don't have is a lot of time.

And if you did find some time, you'd pick up a real book by Elizabeth Peters or Tom Clancy, kick back, and enjoy yourself.

Who wants to read about computers?

Not me, that's for sure. I'm a lot like you. I love my digital camera. I look forward to sharing my pictures, but I don't want to spend hours "playing" with them. I spend enough time sitting at a computer when I'm working—when it comes to my family photos, vacation snapshots, and eBay listing photos, I just want to get them looking good as quickly as possible so that I can get on with my life.

And that's exactly where Photoshop Elements fits into my plans. Now, I'm a huge fan of Big Photoshop's power and breadth of features. It's just that, as mentioned earlier, I don't feel like getting out the big guns after hours. But I'm used to the power of Photoshop—after all, it's the industry standard image editor, and there's just not much it can't do. Given that, is it really possible for Photoshop Elements to keep me happy?

The answer, it turns out, is emphatically yes. With Photoshop Elements, you get maximum results with minimum effort. And version 7 offers more of the same, only better, with three different edit modes, including Guided Edit, which actually teaches you how to use Photoshop Elements right in the program. Photoshop Elements 7 also includes the following:

- A Smart Brush tool that enables you to paint in special effects on separate layers so that you can edit them later

- A Detail Smart Brush that's especially designed for working in small areas without slopping outside the lines

- An enhanced Organizer where you can create photo albums that automatically update your Web galleries when you import appropriate photos and that can back themselves up, too

- The new Photoshop.com Web service, a free way to share your photos online, access and edit your photos from any Web browser, and back up your photos instantly, so that you never risk losing a single pixel

In addition, a pack of built-in wizards do all the heavy lifting involved in creating everything from photo album pages and greeting cards to wall calendars and Web galleries.

So, here's hoping that you love Photoshop Elements as much as I do—and that this book enables you to use the program to create images you'll love even more.

May you enjoy this book, thrill as I did at the tricks you can do with Photoshop Elements, and not spend a minute more than you need to with either of them.

part 1

LEARNING THE ROPES

Back when ships needed favorable winds to get anywhere, new recruits had to learn which ropes to pull to carry out the captain's orders and set sail. This first Part of the book is for novice sailors—people who feel more comfortable if they can begin at the beginning, while their ship is still safely docked. Just turn the page to sign on for a brief orientation session: You'll quickly learn the commands, controls, and features of the Photoshop Elements 7 work area. For example, you'll find out what a *tool* is and how to choose one from the *toolbox*. After you have your bearings, we can use shorthand for the steps in later Parts and just say, "Click the **Crop** tool," and move on.

If you're feeling adventurous, don't worry about sailing ahead to another Part in the book. You can do most of the tasks in any order, and you can always come back to this Part if somehow you get turned around.

Welcome aboard, and fear not: You have nothing to lose but your old film cameras and the long wait for your prints to come back from the lab.

THE PHOTOSHOP ELEMENTS WORK AREA

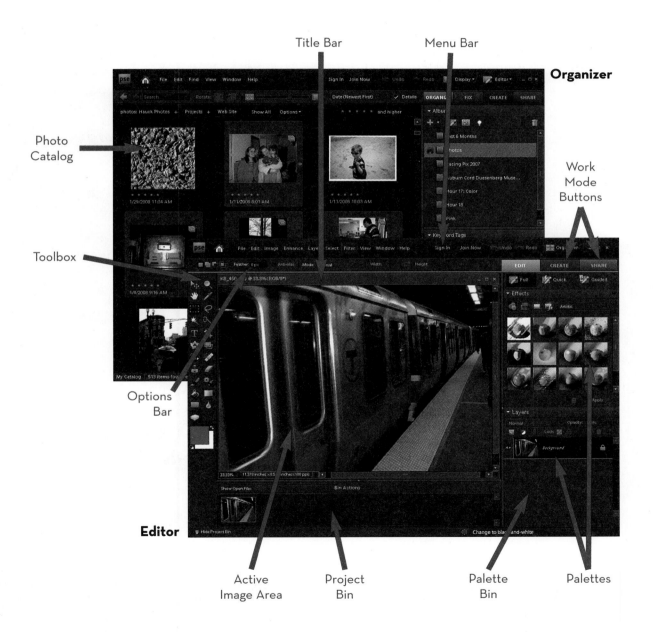

Title Bar

Menu Bar

Organizer

Photo
Catalog

Work
Mode
Buttons

Toolbox

Options
Bar

Editor

Active
Image Area

Project
Bin

Palette
Bin

Palettes

STARTING PHOTOSHOP ELEMENTS

Photoshop Elements has four working modes: Organize, Edit, Create, and Share. To use any of these, you first have to start Elements. The Welcome screen then offers you a path to the mode you want to use.

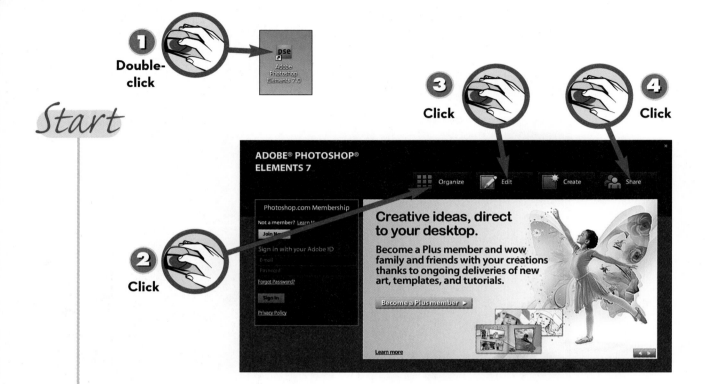

Start

End

(1) Double-click the **Adobe Photoshop Elements 7.0** icon on the Windows Desktop to start the program.

(2) Click the **Organize** button to search your photo collection or import new images from your scanner or camera.

(3) Click the **Edit** button to work on an existing photo.

(4) Click the **Create** or **Share** button to design photo projects, order prints, or put your photos online.

NOTE

More Than a Free Sample

In addition to offering buttons to take you into each different work mode, the Welcome screen invites you to join Photoshop.com, a free Web service that enables you to store and organize your photos online without leaving Photoshop Elements. After you've gotten started with Photoshop.com, you can access your entire photo collection from any Web browser. Give it a try!

OPENING A PHOTO FILE

To access photos that are already in your collection, you use the Organizer, the part of Photoshop Elements that handles the program's Organize, Create, and Share functions. To work on photos that aren't part of your collection, you open them directly from the Editor.

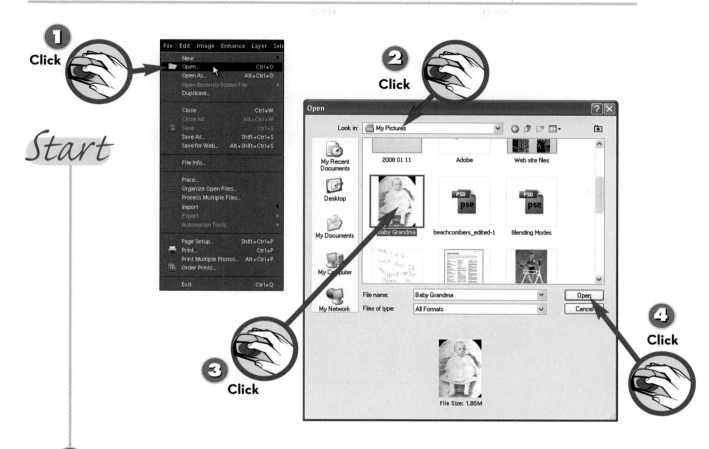

Start

End

1 Choose **File**, **Open**.

2 Navigate to the folder where your image files are stored.

3 Click the file you want to open.

4 Click the **Open** button. The picture opens in the active image area.

TIP
What Can't It Open?
Photoshop Elements 7 can open files in all the following formats: Photoshop, BMP, Camera Raw, GIF, Photo Project Format, EPS, Filmstrip, JPEG, JPEG 2000, PCX, PDF, Photoshop Raw, PICT, Pixar, PNG, Scitex CT, Targa, TIFF, and Wireless Bitmap.

NOTE
To Organize or Not to Organize?
Do you need to store your photos in Organizer? Absolutely not. If you have another way of organizing your photos that you're happy with, by all means stick with it. That said, Organizer is well designed, with a lot of neat features, so it's worth looking it over to see whether it suits your needs.

CATALOGING YOUR PHOTOS IN ORGANIZER

Before you can access any of the Organizer's exciting features, you must get your existing photos into an Organizer catalog. This is an easy process—just tell Organizer where the image files are located, and Elements takes it from there.

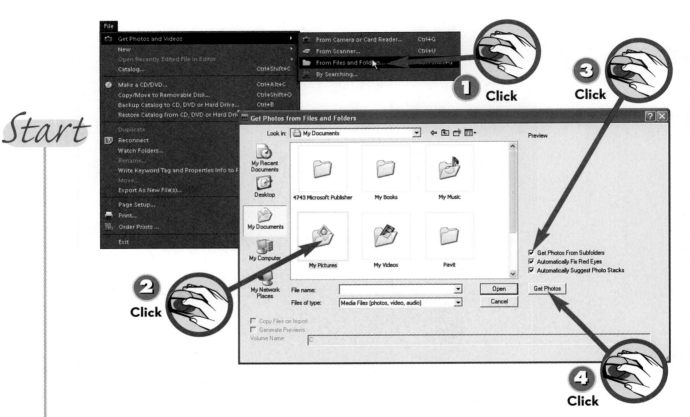

Start

1. In the Organizer, choose **File**, **Get Photos and Videos**, **From Files and Folders**; alternatively, press **Ctrl+Shift+G**.

2. Navigate to the folder that contains your pictures, and click its thumbnail or filename.

3. Click the **Get Photos from Subfolders** and **Automatically Suggest Photo Stacks** check boxes.

4. Click the **Get Photos** button.

Continued

NOTE

Where Do Photos Come From?

The Organizer is also the route that photos take on their way from your digital camera into your computer. To learn more, turn to Part 2, "Getting It All Together."

TIP

Doing More with Organizer

You can group your photos into albums, assign keywords to them, and even have Photoshop Elements pick out all the faces they contain so that you can add IDs for people. To learn how to make the most of Organizer, turn to Part 10, "Organizing and Presenting Your Photos."

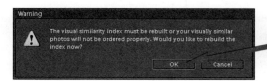

5 If you see a warning dialog, click **OK** to index the catalog.

6 If your catalog needed indexing, click **OK** when the catalog indexing is complete.

7 Click **Stack All Groups** to organize similar photos into stacks.

8 Click **OK**. The photos in the folder are added to a new catalog.

End

-NOTE-
I'm Organized, Now What?
Now that your photos are in Organizer, what do you do with them? Start by clicking any photo and then clicking the **Fix**, **Create**, or **Share** buttons at the top of the window to edit or create a project with that photo.

-TIP-
Another Way of Looking at Things
Choose **Date View** from the Display menu at the top of the window to see the photos you took each day in a month or a year. Click **Next Item on Selected Day** at the right side of the window to scroll through the photos for a day.

STARTING WITH A BLANK CANVAS

Not all images start out as photographs. Sometimes you just want to paint or draw. For that to happen, you need to start with a blank document rather than opening an existing file. You can choose the size and resolution of your new image file.

Start

Click

Click

(1) If you're in the Organizer, choose **Editor**, **Full Edit** from the menu bar to switch to Full Edit mode.

(2) In the Editor, choose **File**, **New**, **Blank File** or press **Ctrl+N**.

Continued

NOTE

The Color of the Canvas

You can choose a background color for your new image from the Background Contents pop-up menu. White gives you a blank white "page" to draw on, and Background Color makes the canvas whatever color is the current background color in the toolbox. Transparent enables you to overlay your drawing on another image.

TIP

Sizing for a Copied Image

If an image is on the Clipboard, Photoshop Elements automatically inserts the size and resolution of that image in the New dialog box. Click **OK**; then press **Ctrl+V** to paste the image into the document.

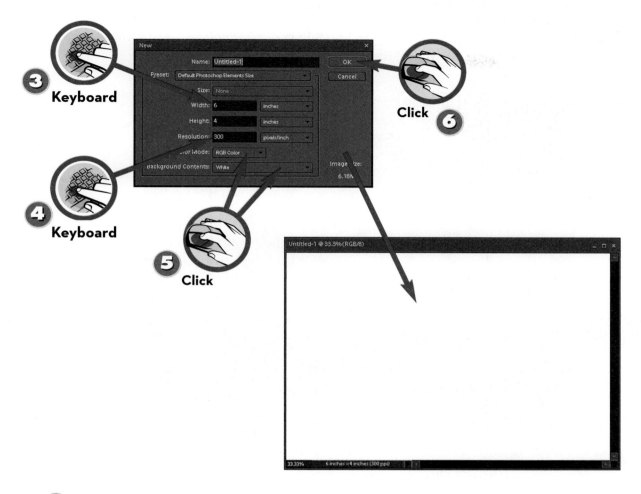

3 Keyboard

4 Keyboard

5 Click

6 Click

---

3 Enter Width and Height values for the new file.

4 Choose a Resolution value.

5 Set the Color Mode to **RGB Color** and choose an option from the Background Contents menu.

6 Click **OK** to create the new file. A blank image window opens.

End

TIP

Resolved: Choosing a Resolution

Resolution refers to how many pixels—tiny, square image elements—per inch there are in your image. Higher resolution values enable you to print an image at larger sizes without the image becoming blocky. When you're creating a new image file, enter **72 ppi** in the Resolution field for an image that you plan to display only onscreen, or a higher value such as 300 ppi for an image you plan to print out.

CHANGING YOUR VIEW

When you have a picture file open for editing, you'll usually want to make it as large as possible onscreen. This gives you the clearest overall view, regardless of the actual image size. Then, you can use the Zoom tool (or the Zoom In command in the View menu) to magnify small areas if you need to work in even finer detail.

Start

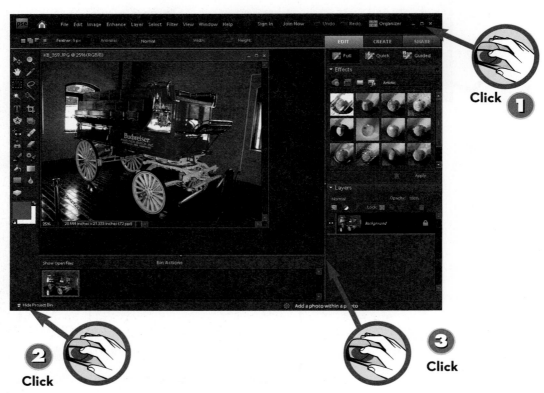

Click **1**

Click **2**

3 Click

1 In the Editor, click the program window's **Maximize** button so that the Elements window fills the entire screen.

2 To clear the work area, click the arrow to hide the Project Bin, if it's open.

3 Click the border between the image area and the Palette Bin to close it, if it's open.

Continued

TIP

Zoom Zoom

If you want to see a larger preview of a photo in Organizer, double-click its thumbnail. To switch back to the main Organizer window, click the **Back** button at the left end of the toolbar.

4 **Click**

5 **Click and drag**

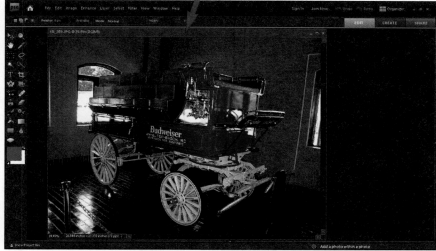

4 From the menu bar, choose **View**, **Fit on Screen** or press **Ctrl+0** (zero). The active image window enlarges to fill the work area.

5 Click and drag the active image window's title bar to move the window around.

End

TIP

Open Windows

You can have more than one picture open at the same time. Choose a picture for editing by clicking its title bar to make its window active. (If you can't see all the title bars, choose **Window**, **Images**, **Cascade** to see them all.)

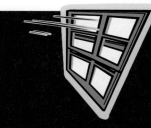

CHOOSING TOOLS FROM THE TOOLBOX

The tools in the Editor's toolbox help you work on portions of a picture in a variety of ways. For example, the Zoom tool enlarges your view of a picture. Different edit modes (Full Edit, Quick Edit, and Guided Edit) have different tool sets, but each mode has a toolbox.

Start

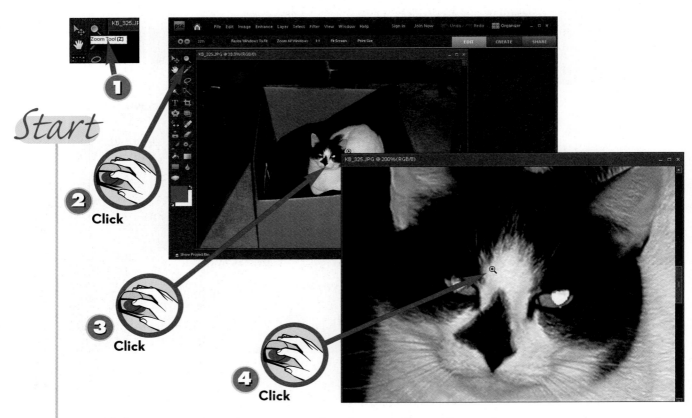

1 Click

2 Click

3 Click

4 Click

1 Hold the pointer over the Zoom tool without clicking. The tool's name appears in a tool tip, along with its shortcut key.

2 Click the **Zoom** tool or press **Z**. The pointer changes to a magnifying glass symbol, and settings that affect the tool appear in the options bar.

3 Move the pointer to the center of the area you want enlarged, and click. A magnified view appears in the active image area.

4 Click again and again to enlarge the view in progressive steps. The magnification percentage appears in the title bar.

Continued

NOTE

Zoom In

Zooming doesn't make any changes to the picture itself, just to your view of it in Photoshop Elements so that you can work on fine details.

TIP

Shortcut

When using the Zoom tool, right-click anywhere within the active image area and choose **Fit on Screen** to quickly view the entire image without having to scroll.

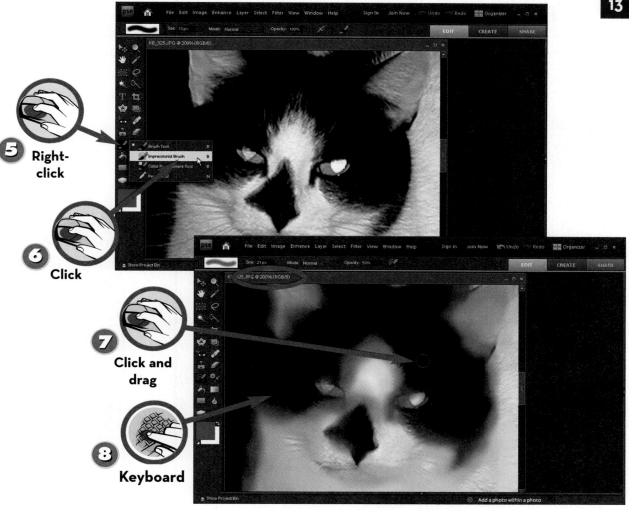

5 Right-click the **Brush** tool to view all the available brush tools.

6 Switch to the **Impressionist Brush** tool. The pointer changes to the brush tip, and settings for the tool appear in the options bar.

7 Move the pointer to the area of the picture where you want to use the brush, and then click and drag it around, as if painting, to apply the effect.

8 Because you made a change to the picture, press **Ctrl+S** to save your work.

End

TIP

Best-Quality Image

After you've made changes to a JPEG file, for best quality you should use the **File**, **Save As** command to convert it to TIFF (.tif) format or save it as a Photoshop (.psd) file.

NOTE

Two, Two, Two (Or More) Tools in One

The toolbar contains 23 slots, but it has a lot more tools than that. Any tool icon with a triangle next to it is actually a pop-up menu holding two or more related tools.

SETTING TOOL OPTIONS

After you click to choose a tool from the Editor's toolbox, you can change settings in the options bar that control its effect. Let's try it with the Horizontal Type tool.

Start

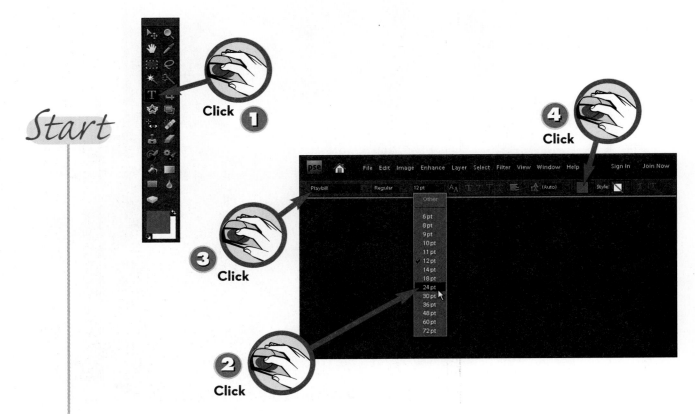

1. In the toolbox, click the **Horizontal Type** tool, or press **T**. Settings for the tool appear in the options bar.

2. Choose a Font Style and Font Size from the pop-up menus in the options bar.

3. Use the Font pop-up menu to choose a new font for your text, such as Playbill.

4. Click the **Text Color** swatch. The Color Picker opens.

Continued

TIP

Click Reset

The first button on the options bar has the same icon as whatever tool you're using. Click it to see a pop-up menu you can use to reset the options for the current tool or for all tools.

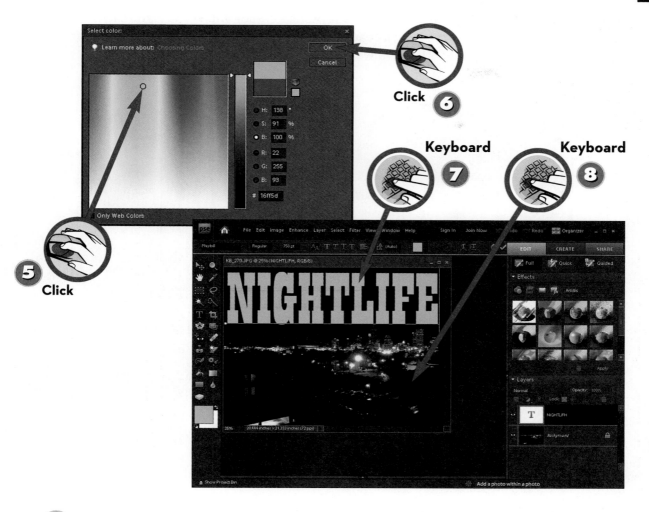

Click **5**

Click **6**

Keyboard **7**

Keyboard **8**

5 In the Color Picker, click in the color space to choose a color.

6 Click **OK**.

7 Click in the image window and type some text, such as **NIGHTLIFE**.

8 Press **Ctrl+S** to save your work.

End

NOTE

Settings Retained

Settings you make in the options bar remain in effect for a particular tool until you change them again, even if you quit and then restart the program.

USING CONTEXTUAL MENUS

Contextual menus pop up at the tip of your mouse cursor when you right-click in the image window. They're contextual because their contents change depending on which tool you're using, so the commands are always appropriate to their context.

Right-click ①

Right-click ②

Right-click ③

Start

End

① With any selection tool active, right-click in the image area to see a menu of selection commands.

② With a painting tool active, right-click in the image area to see a menu of brush shapes.

③ With the Custom Shape tool active (its icon is shaped like a heart), right-click in the image area to see a menu of drawing shapes.

-NOTE-
Keeping Things in Context
Try right-clicking with each tool to see all the contextual menus Photoshop Elements has to offer. Using them is a real time-saver.

-TIP-
Layer by Layer
When you're building layered images (see Part 6, "Using Layers to Combine Photos and Artwork," to learn more), you can quickly switch layers by right-clicking with the Move tool or a selection tool.

SWITCHING EDIT MODES

The Photoshop Elements Editor has three working modes. In Full Edit mode, all tools and palettes are available to you. In Quick Fix mode, the program's interface is stripped down to just the controls you need to apply fast, automated edits. And in Guided Edit mode, Photoshop Elements provides step-by-step instructions for using its tools and commands.

1 After starting up Photoshop Elements, click the **Edit** button on the Welcome screen to open the Editor.

2 When you're in Quick Fix or Guided Edit mode, click the **Full** button to switch to Full Edit mode.

3 When you're in Full Edit or Guided Edit mode, click the **Quick** button to switch to Quick Fix mode.

4 When you're in Full Edit or Quick Fix mode, click the **Guided** button to switch to Guided Edit mode.

TIP
Fixing It Quickly
You can still make quick fixes when you're in Full Edit mode. You can use the Auto commands in the Enhance menu to adjust color, lighting, and contrast (or choose **Enhance, Auto Smart Fix** to adjust everything simultaneously).

USING PALETTES

Palettes, floating windows that contain help and commands grouped by category, are a truly handy feature. For example, the Info palette shows color values and measurements for the current image or selected area.

Start

1 Click

2 Click

Click and drag

3

4 Click

① In the Editor's Full Edit mode, choose a palette name from the Window menu to open a palette. This example uses the Info palette.

② Click the palette's **More** button (or the double-triangle button, if the palette is docked) to see a menu of commands related to the palette's function.

③ Drag the palette's title bar to move it around the screen.

④ Click the palette's close box to dismiss the palette.

End

NOTE
Getting More
The options in the palette menu differ for each palette. Be sure to check them all so that you know which features you can access via each palette's menu.

TIP
Layer Info
Especially as you begin to combine images or create artwork from them, get in the habit of leaving the Layers palette open. As you add text, graphics, painting, or images, you'll quickly see why keeping track of layers is important.

STORING PALETTES

Floating palettes are great, but they take up a lot of space on your screen. The Palette Bin on the right side of your screen is a handy place to stash palettes so that they don't obscure your view of the image you're working on.

Start

1 Click   **2** Click   **3** Click and drag

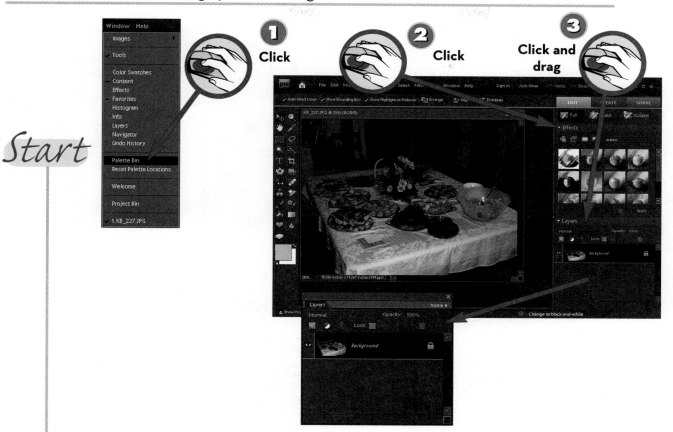

1 In Full Edit mode, choose **Window**, **Palette Bin** to open the bin if it's not already visible.

2 Click the disclosure triangle in the title bar of a palette in the Palette Bin to expand or shrink the palette.

3 Drag a palette's title bar to remove it from the Palette Bin.

End

SETTING YOUR OWN PREFERENCES

These steps show you where to look if you want to customize how Photoshop Elements shows things in the work area, how it saves files, and other options. As just one of many options, these steps explain how to change the unit of measure in the work area from inches to centimeters.

Start

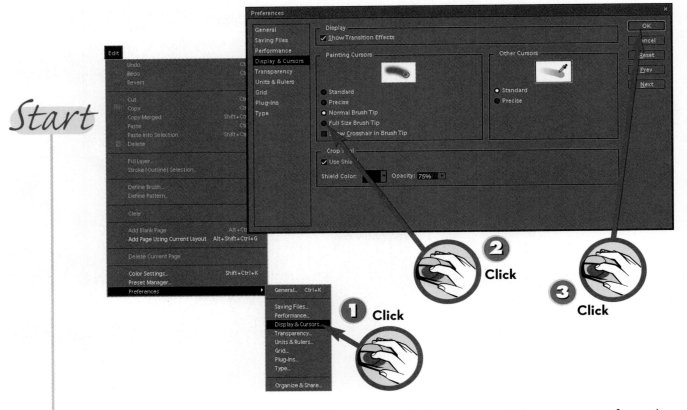

1 From the menu bar, choose **Edit**, **Preferences** and choose one of the categories from the submenu.

2 Set the options you want to change. For example, click **Full Size Brush Tip** in the Painting Cursors area to make your brush cursor extend to the full size of your current brush tip.

3 Click **OK**.

End

NOTE

Default Settings

Default preference settings should work fine for most people. Experiment with the settings as you get more comfortable with Photoshop Elements. If you're always having to change a setting manually, you might find you can improve your efficiency by changing a preference.

SAVING YOUR WORK

All the work you do on a picture in Photoshop Elements will be lost unless you save the file to disk. If you are saving a file for the first time, you can simply press **Ctrl+S** on the keyboard. If you need to save a file to another location or under a new name, these steps show you how.

Start

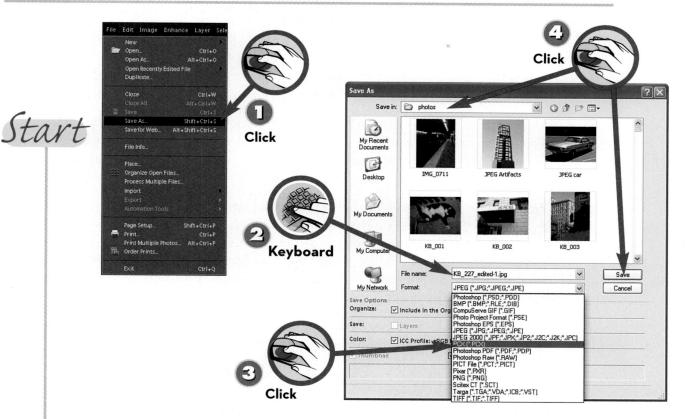

End

① To save a file to a different drive or folder or with a different name, choose **File**, **Save As** from the menu bar or press **Shift+Ctrl+S**.

② Type a name for the new file. (You don't have to type the filename extension, such as .jpg.)

③ Optionally, choose an option from the Format pop-up menu to change the file type.

④ Use the Save In pop-up menu to store the file in a different folder or on a different drive. Click **Save**.

NOTE

File Types

You can keep digital snapshots in the format the camera makes, usually JPEG (.jpg) files. If you plan to make changes to them, however, it's better to save them as Photoshop (.psd) files.

NOTE

Digital Negatives

If your computer can burn CDs, it's a good idea to save your unedited camera originals to discs. These are your digital "negatives." That way, if you make changes to an image on your hard drive, you still have a copy of the untouched original.

GETTING IT ALL TOGETHER

In this Part, you'll learn how to get pictures into your computer so that you can work with them in Photoshop Elements.

After all, you can't do much of anything with your pictures until they exist as digital files on your computer's hard drive. Photos you take with your digital camera, DV camcorder, or camera phone are already stored as digital files, but you must transfer them from the camera's internal storage to your hard drive.

You can also work with film shots—prints, negatives, and slides—but you must *digitize* them first. That's what a scanner does. It scans a print with a beam of light, breaking the image into a collection of individual colored dots, or *pixels* (picture elements). All digital images are composed of pixels, and the main thing Photoshop Elements does is help you change the colors of thousands or even millions of pixels at once, in interesting and useful ways.

Whether you use the other tasks in this book to work with your shots a little or a lot, you'll also learn how to create finished images as prints or contact sheets.

THE INS AND OUTS OF DIGITAL PHOTOGRAPHY

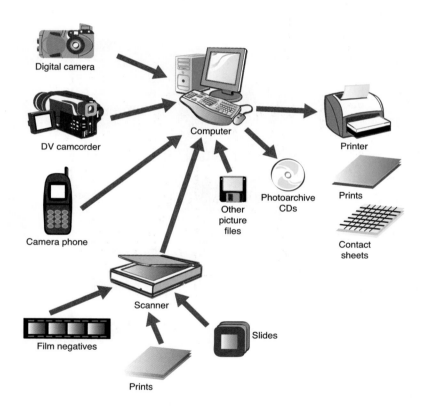

Digital camera

DV camcorder

Camera phone

Computer

Printer

Prints

Contact sheets

Other picture files

Photoarchive CDs

Scanner

Film negatives

Prints

Slides

MOVING IMAGES FROM CAMERA TO COMPUTER

Most digital cameras and camera phones come with their own software for browsing image files and uploading them to your computer. However, you can use the steps described here to transfer files from most picture-taking devices using Photoshop Elements built-in functions.

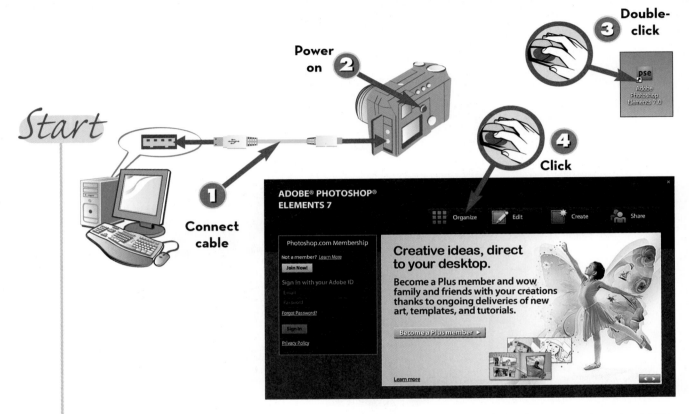

1. Connect the smaller end of the data cable to the camera and the larger end to the USB port of your computer.

2. Turn the camera's power on.

3. Double-click the program icon on the Windows Desktop to start Photoshop Elements.

4. In the Welcome screen, click **Organize**.

Continued

 TIP

Getting There from Here

If you're already working in the Editor when you want to import photos, click the **Organizer** button in the menu bar to switch to Organizer.

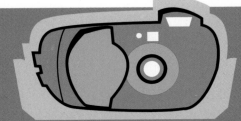

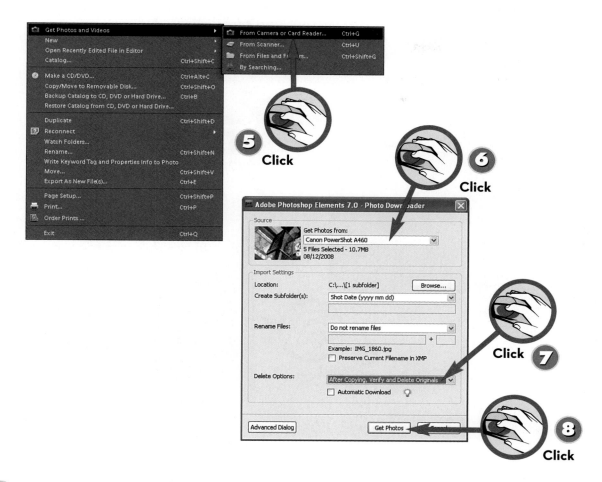

5 Choose **File, Get Photos and Videos, From Camera or Card Reader**.

6 Choose your camera from the Get Photos From pop-up menu.

7 Choose a setting from the Delete Options pop-up menu.

8 Click **Get Photos**.

End

TIP

What's in a Name?

If you like to use filenames to identify photos (such as when you're printing contact sheets), check the **Rename Files To** box and type a word or two in the text entry field. Elements renames the imported images with that text, plus a sequential number.

NOTE

Alphabet Soup

Cameras generate filenames automatically. For example, Pmmddoooo.jpg, where P = still photo, mm = the month, dd = the day, and oooo = an image number.

SCANNING IMAGES

Scanning and storing your old snapshots in your computer is not only a wonderful way to reduce clutter and organize those shoeboxes full of prints—Photoshop Elements also has lots of ways to bring back faded color, touch up complexions, and even erase uninvited guests.

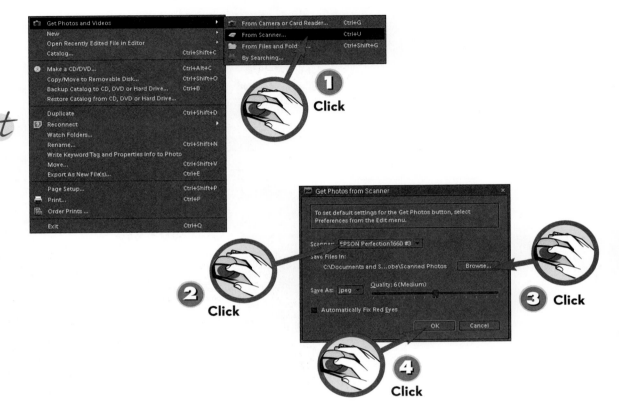

1 In Organizer, choose **File**, **Get Photos and Videos**, **From Scanner**.

2 Choose your scanner from the Scanner pop-up menu.

3 Click **Browse** if you want to choose another location for the image file that Photoshop Elements will create, and set its File Type and Quality (if saving as JPEG).

4 Click **OK**.

Continued

NOTE
Adding to Your Collection
These steps create a file automatically and add it to your photo collection in Organizer, which displays only the new photo. Click the **Back** button at the top of the Organizer window to return to viewing your entire collection.

TIP
Where'd It Go?
Photoshop Elements stores scanned images in a folder by themselves, because it doesn't have any information on where they came from. To place a scanned image in a different folder, click the **Browse** button in the Get Photos from Scanner dialog and choose a different location.

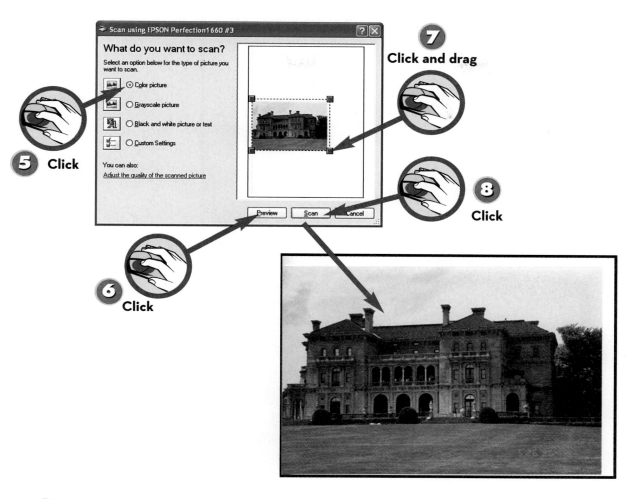

5 Choose the kind of picture you want to scan.

6 Click **Preview**.

7 Click and drag a corner of the marquee that appears around the image on the scanner bed to adjust the area of the image that will actually be scanned, if needed.

8 Click **Scan**. The scanned print appears in the active image area, ready for editing.

End

TIP

Scanning Secrets

The dialog boxes that you see in step 5 might look different, depending on your scanner model. When choosing a picture type, choose grayscale to capture shading. For photos you might want to print later, click **Custom Settings** and set the resolution to 300 dpi.

TIP

Crop Now, Crop Later

When you're scanning, you can adjust the marquee in the preview scan so that you scan only the part of the image you want. Don't bring the marquee in *too* close; it's better to have to crop an image again in the Editor than to risk clipping off part of the image when scanning.

GRABBING A VIDEO FRAME

Photoshop Elements can't capture still photos from uploaded DV files (digital video files with the .mov extension), but you can follow these steps to capture one or more stills as your camcorder plays back recorded video, which achieves the same result.

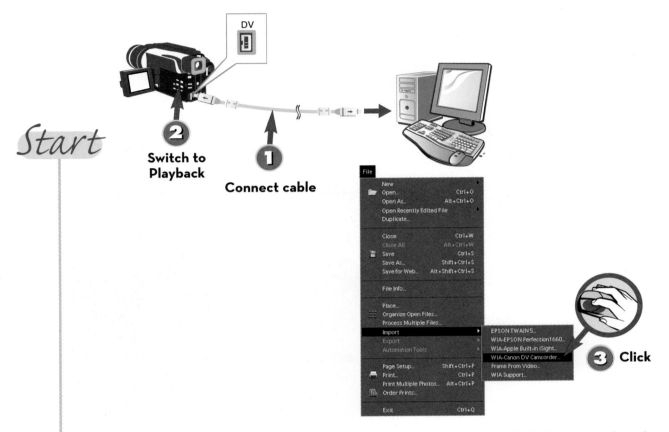

Start

Switch to Playback

Connect cable

Click

1. Connect the smaller end of the data cable to the camcorder, and the larger end to the USB or FireWire port of your computer.

2. Switch the camcorder to Playback (or VCR) mode.

3. In the Editor, choose **File**, **Import**, **WIA <*camera name*>**. Press **Play** on the camcorder to start the video playback.

Continued

NOTE

A Note on Quality

Don't be surprised if the video still images look fuzzy; because it takes so many images to make up just a few seconds of video, these shots are taken at a rather low resolution. You don't generally notice it on the TV screen, but it becomes apparent when you grab still images.

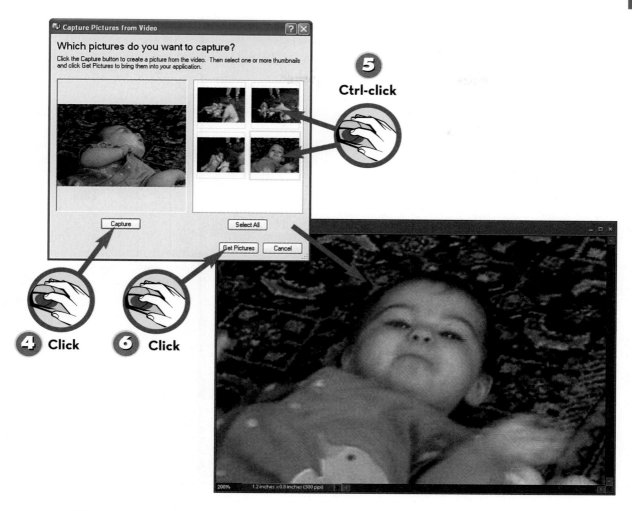

 Ctrl-click

4 Click   **6 Click**

4 Video plays in the preview area on the left. When you see the frame you want, click **Capture**. (Repeat this step to capture other frames.)

5 Press **Ctrl** while you click each thumbnail you want (or click **Select All** to get all of them).

6 Click **Get Pictures**. The video stills open for editing in separate windows in the work area.

End

TIP
Other Options
For these steps to work with your camcorder, it must be a WIA (Windows Image Acquisition) device. If you have an older DV (Digital Video) camcorder, upload the clips as video files, use a video editor such as Pinnacle Studio to save as a Windows movie (.wmv), and then choose **File**, **Import**, **Frame from Video** instead.

CAUTION
You Must Remember This
Don't forget to click to select all the images you want to bring into Photoshop Elements in the Capture Pictures dialog box. If you don't, only the last frame you captured will be saved; the others will be deleted.

OPENING A PICTURE FROM THE CLIPBOARD

The Windows *Clipboard* is a reserved area of your computer's memory designed specifically for exchanging data—such as photos, drawings, or text—among applications. For example, you can open a document in Microsoft Word, select one of the pictures in it, and copy the image into Photoshop Elements.

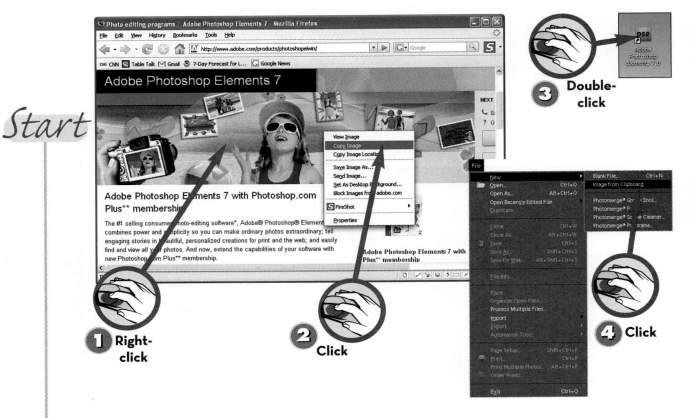

Start

1 Right-click

2 Click

3 Double-click

4 Click

1. In another application, such as Mozilla Firefox, right-click the image you want.

2. From the contextual menu, choose **Copy Image** or press **Ctrl+C**.

3. Start Photoshop Elements (or switch to it if it's already open).

4. From the Photoshop Elements menu bar (either the Editor or Organizer), choose **File**, **New**, **Image from Clipboard**. A copy of the picture opens in the active image window for editing.

End

TIP

Native Files

The copied image comes into Photoshop Elements in whatever format it was in the original document; but if you edit it and then try to save, the program prompts you to save it as a native Photoshop (.psd) file. Saving a copy of your image as a PSD file is a good idea because it enables you to continue making edits to the file. If you save as another format, such as JPG or GIF, the changes you make are incorporated into the file, and you can no longer undo them.

RESIZING AND PRINTING AN IMAGE

Photoshop Elements reports the current print size of the image in the lower-left corner of the work area. With these few steps, you can resize the image to fit exactly on the printed page. This method uses the default paper size currently set for your printer.

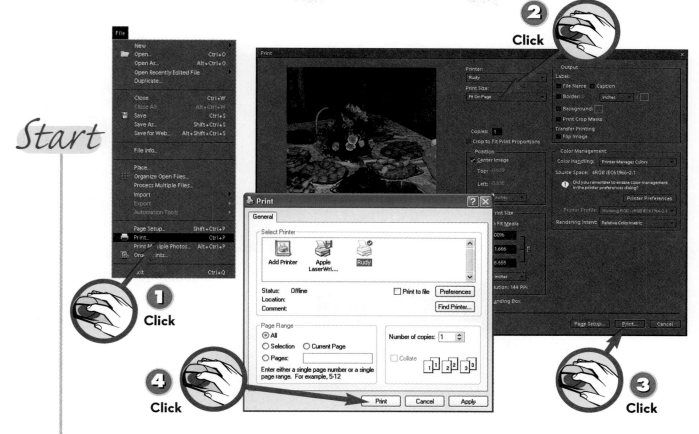

Start

End

1. From the Photoshop Elements menu bar, choose **File**, **Print**.

2. Choose **Fit on Page** from the Print Size pop-up menu.

3. Click **Print**.

4. Click **Print** again in the Print dialog box.

TIP
Switch Orientations
The default printer orientation is Portrait (long side vertical). To switch to Landscape (long side horizontal), after step 2 click the **Page Setup** button, choose **Landscape**, click **OK**, and then go to step 3.

NOTE
Glossy Prints
For the best-quality prints on a color inkjet printer, use glossy photo paper. Remove the plain paper and feed just one sheet at a time, because the glossy surface can stick to other sheets and cause jams.

ADDING A WHITE BORDER TO YOUR PRINTS

A good way to add a white border to your prints, even when you're using a borderless printer, involves resizing the image to be smaller than the canvas (paper) size by the amount of the margin you want and then centering the image on the canvas.

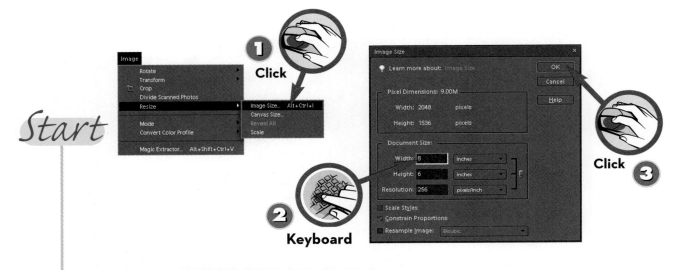

1 With a picture open in the Editor, choose **Image**, **Resize**, **Image Size**.

2 Type the new image width, such as **8** inches.

3 Click **OK**.

4 Choose **Image**, **Resize**, **Canvas Size**.

Continued

TIP

When to Resample

In step 2, check **Resample Image** and increase the resolution if the number in the Resolution field is less than 150. To avoid distorting the image, let the program calculate the height.

TIP

Yet Another Way

To add a white border without resizing the canvas, choose **File**, **Print Preview**. Check the **Show More Options** check box; then click the **Border** button. You can specify the width of the border in inches, millimeters, or points.

5 Keyboard

6 Keyboard

7 Click

8 Click

5 In the Width box, type the width of the print paper—larger than the image width—such as **8.5** inches.

6 In the Height box, type the height of the paper, such as **6.5** inches.

7 Click **OK**.

8 Load the printer with photo paper and choose **File**, **Print**. You'll need to click **Print** in the Print dialog.

End

NOTE
Note the Printable Area
The border becomes part of the image file, so you shouldn't have to adjust print margins as long as the *printable area* of your paper matches the canvas size. Use the steps in this task to add borders to the pictures you print with Picture Package, which uses standard print sizes.

NOTE
What's the Anchor Point?
The *anchor point* indicates the position of the image relative to the canvas edges. The default anchor point is Centered.

PRINTING CONTACT SHEETS

Professional photographers routinely make contact sheets by printing negatives laid directly on photosensitive paper. Photoshop Elements will generate contact sheets that automatically show thumbnails with labels of any group of files you select.

1 Click

Start

2 Ctrl-click

3 Click

1 If you're working in the Editor, click the **Organizer** button to switch to Organizer.

2 Select the photos you want to include in the contact sheet. Press the **Ctrl** key while clicking images to select multiple images simultaneously.

3 Choose **File**, **Print** or press **Ctrl+P**.

Continued

NOTE

Get the Contact

Print and store contact sheets with each of your photo archive CDs. It's a handy way of browsing the images when they're no longer on your hard drive.

TIP

Preview First

Save paper by using the preview area in the Print Selected Photos dialog box to see how many photos appear on the last page of your contact sheets. If there's just one or two, consider reducing the number of columns.

4 Choose a printer from the Select Printer pop-up menu.

5 Choose **Contact Sheet** from the Select Type of Print pop-up menu.

6 Choose a layout, based on the size you want the photos to be on the contact sheet.

7 Load your printer with photo paper and click **Print**.

End

NOTE
Useful Captions

For more descriptive captions, rename camera files in Windows Explorer or in Organizer before you generate the contact sheets.

TIP
Out of a Jam

The thumbnails of the selected files won't necessarily fit on a single contact sheet. If they don't, Photoshop Elements will print multiple sheets. Remember, to avoid printer jams, load photo paper manually, one sheet at a time.

PRINTING A PICTURE PACKAGE

Professional photographers who shoot annual school photos, weddings, and social events offer their subjects *picture packages*, prints ranging from wallet size to 8 × 10s for framing. Photoshop Elements will print a variety of assorted sizes for you on a sheet of photo paper. It's sure to please your "customers."

1 Click

Start

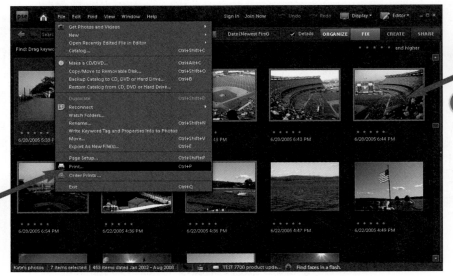

2 Ctrl-click

3 Click

1 If you're working in the Editor, click the **Organizer** button to switch to Organizer.

2 Select one or more photos to include in the picture package.

3 Choose **File**, **Print** or press **Ctrl+P**.

Continued

NOTE

Just Like a Pro

Have your subjects pick the shots they want from a contact sheet, and then make up their picture packages. Use bright-white, glossy photo paper, and feed one sheet at a time to avoid printer jams.

NOTE

Paper for Your Printer

When you shop for photo paper, you'll see dozens of brands and types. For best quality, go with the brand that matches your printer and the thickest paper. (Paper is measured in mils; you want 9 or 10 mil.) The paper's finish—glossy or matte—is strictly a matter of personal preference.

4 Choose a printer from the Select Printer pop-up menu.

5 Choose **Picture Package** from the Select Type of Print pop-up menu.

6 Choose a layout. If you're printing just one photo, check the box marked **Fill Page with First Photo**.

7 Load your printer with photo paper and click **Print**.

End

 TIP
Choose Your Size
If you're printing more than one photo, drag the photos in the preview area to change which photo is used for each size the layout includes.

 TIP
Getting Framed
Don't forget to try the frame options available for picture package layouts. They range from actual frames (such as Country) to sophisticated edge treatments (such as Painted Edge).

BASIC PHOTO FIXING

Think of this Part of the book as a comfy family restaurant where you can go for your daily bread and never be bored with the same meal twice. It's just not slick, or complicated, or arty. (Oh, we'll go there, too, eventually.) You'd be well served to return here again and again—but these steps are so quick and easy that to do them once is to know them cold.

Up to this point, you've opened files and printed them out, but you haven't changed how they look very much. If you need to fix a photo, come here first. Your quest will probably end here, and you'll be more than satisfied. The shot that looked too dark will perk right up, crooked will become straight, and that unflattering pallor on your subject's face will become a rosy glow.

A particularly handy feature of Photoshop Elements is the Quick Fix workspace, which gives you single-click access to a variety of commonly needed repairs—with automatic corrections. The first several tasks in this part demonstrate its use.

So, if you have time to do only a few of the tasks in this book, choose some of these. You'll be hooked, and you'll recover a lot of shots you thought were duds.

APPLYING QUICK AND EASY FIXES

Before

After

MAKING GENERAL QUICK FIXES

You can use Photoshop Elements Quick Fix mode as one-stop-shopping for all the commands in the Enhance menu. You can get there by clicking the **Edit** button on the Welcome screen or by choosing **Editor**, **Quick Fix** button at the top right of the Organizer window.

Click

Start

Click

Click

Click

Click

1 With the picture you want to fix open in the Editor, click the **Quick** button at the top of the Palette Bin.

2 Click the disclosure triangle for the section you want to use (such as Lighting).

3 Click an **Auto** button (such as the one for Levels) to adjust the image; Levels adjusts the picture's balance of dark and light areas.

4 If you don't like the changes Elements makes, click **Reset** to restore the image to its original state.

End

NOTE
Auto and Semi-Auto Fixes
Any of the Auto adjustments require just a single click of the button. If you want more control over the changes being made to your image, you can use the sliders to determine the amount of modification made to lighting and color and the amount of sharpening (see the next task).

TIP
Don't Like *After*?
Your Quick Fix changes are cumulative, so you can do one, such as Auto Lighting, and then do another, such as a custom amount of sharpening applied with the slider—until the *after* image is just right.

UNDOING YOUR MISTAKES

Don't think of any photo-fixing decisions you make as mistakes, for two good reasons: You can always undo them, and experimenting is the only way to learn what works and what doesn't. So, click away—you have nothing to lose but playtime!

Start

End

1 Immediately after making any change to the picture in the Editor, choose **Edit**, **Undo**, or press **Ctrl+Z**.

2 To undo the next-most-recent change, click the **Undo** button (or press **Ctrl+Z**) again.

3 To reapply the last change you undid, choose **Edit**, **Redo** (or press **Ctrl+Y**) before you do anything else.

TIP
Other Ways to Undo
If you want to see everything you've done to an image before you start undoing, you can use the Undo and Redo buttons, or open the Undo History palette (choose **Window**, **Undo History**). Right-click the step you want to undo, and choose **Delete** (subsequent steps are deleted, too).

TIP
Canceling All Changes
To undo all your changes during a session—before you save—choose **Edit**, **Revert**. The last saved version of the file appears in the active image area.

MAKING LIGHTING QUICK FIXES

Photoshop Elements Lighting Quick Fixes are designed to fix images that are too light, too dark, or too grayish. You can bring out shadow detail, tone down harsh highlights, and improve a picture's overall contrast.

Click

Start

Click

Click

1 With the picture you want to fix open in the Editor, click the **Quick** button at the top of the Palette Bin.

2 To have Photoshop Elements even out the dark and light areas in the image, click the **Auto Levels** button in the Lighting area.

3 To have Photoshop Elements adjust the image's contrast, click the **Auto Contrast** button.

Continued

NOTE
Fully Automatic
The Quick Fix Auto buttons for lighting duplicate the function of the Enhance menu commands Auto Levels and Auto Contrast. You can also use keyboard shortcuts for these functions; press **Shift+Ctrl+L** for Auto Levels or **Alt+Shift+Ctrl+L** for Auto Contrast.

TIP
What's in Your Toolbox?
When you're in Quick Fix mode, your toolbox is limited to just a few tools: the Zoom tool, the Hand tool, the Magic Selection tool, and the Crop tool. If you need to use tools that aren't available, switch to Full Edit mode by clicking the Full button at the top of the Palette Bin.

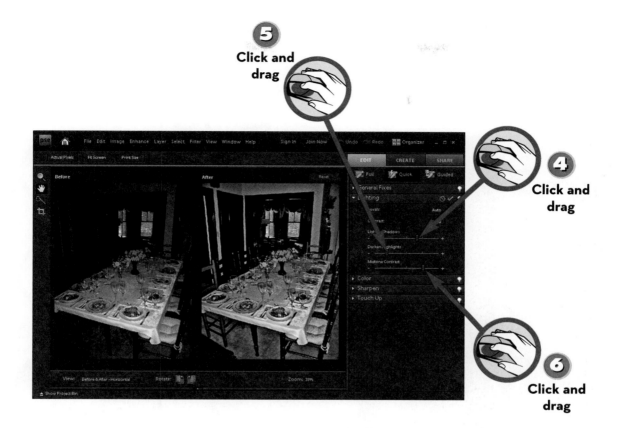

5 Click and drag

4 Click and drag

6 Click and drag

4 To lighten the darkest areas of the picture, click and drag the **Lighten Shadows** slider.

5 To darken the brightest areas of the picture, click and drag the **Darken Highlights** slider.

6 To adjust the image's overall contrast yourself, click and drag the **Midtone Contrast** slider left or right.

End

NOTE

Just the Highlights

To adjust an image's shadows and highlights in Full Edit mode, choose **Enhance**, **Lighting**, **Shadows/Highlights**. The sliders in this dialog are the same as the ones in the Lighting area of the Palette Bin when you're in Quick Fix mode.

MAKING COLOR QUICK FIXES

In the Color section of the Quick Fix mode's Palette Bin, you'll find tools to repair images whose colors are off and even ones that are too colorful or not colorful enough. Try the Auto buttons first. If you don't get the result you're looking for, undo and see what you can do with the four different sliders.

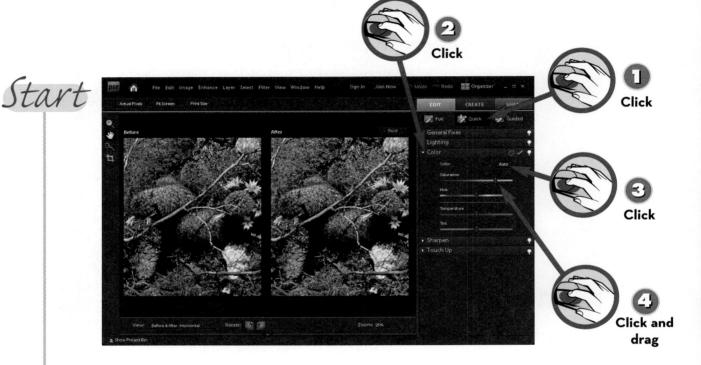

Start

2 Click

1 Click

3 Click

4 Click and drag

1. With the picture you want to fix open in the Editor, click the **Quick** button at the top of the Palette Bin.

2. Click the triangle to reveal the contents of the Color palette.

3. To have Photoshop Elements fix the picture's color, click the **Auto Color** button in the Color area.

4. To make the colors more or less vivid, click and drag the **Saturation** slider.

Continued

NOTE
Polyunsaturated Colors
The term *saturation* refers to the intensity of a color. A completely desaturated color is gray, white, or black.

TIP
The Two *T*'s
You'll find the Tint and Temperature sliders in the Lighting area especially useful for adjusting older photos that have color-shifted over the years, as well as photos taken under artificial lighting.

5 To modify the hues in the picture, click and drag the **Hue** slider left or right.

6 To make the image appear cooler (more blue) or warmer (more red), click and drag the **Temperature** slider.

7 To compensate for a green cast or a pink cast, click and drag the **Tint** slider right or left, respectively.

End

NOTE

It's All About Skin

When you're adjusting color, don't forget to look at the whole image, and concentrate particularly on skin tones. People notice oddities in these parts of a picture more than anywhere else. If you find that you need to adjust color differently in different parts of the picture, switch to Full Edit mode and select each part of the image to work on in turn.

APPLYING QUICK FIX TOUCH-UPS

Most Quick Fixes are applied to the entire image. The tools in the Touch Up area, however, make it possible for you to apply a fix to a specific area. You can remove red eye, whiten teeth, make the gray sky blue, or even turn part of an image grayscale to give the color areas greater punch.

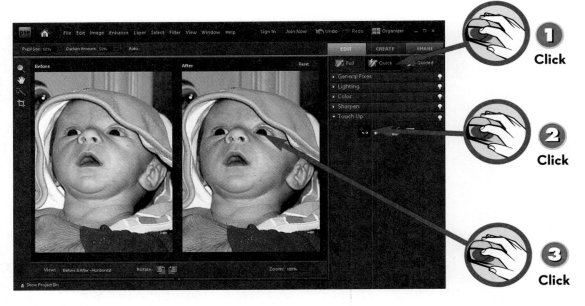

Start

1 With the picture you want to fix open in the Editor, click the **Quick** button at the top of the Palette Bin.

2 Click the **Red Eye Removal** tool in the Touch Up area.

3 Click the eyes in the After view of the image to remove the red eye effect.

Continued

NOTE

What You Want to See

When you're working in Quick Fix mode, you can choose which versions of the picture display onscreen. From the View menu at the bottom of the Palette Bin, choose one of the following: **After Only, Before Only, Before & After - Horizontal, Before & After - Vertical**.

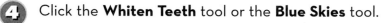

5 Click and drag

4 Click

6 Click

7 Click and drag

4 Click the **Whiten Teeth** tool or the **Blue Skies** tool.

5 Click and drag over teeth to make them whiter or the sky to make it more intensely blue.

6 Click the **Black and White** tool.

7 Click and drag over any part of the image to convert that area to grayscale with high contrast.

End

NOTE
Available 24/7
Several useful functions are always available at the bottom of the Quick Fix window, no matter which tool is active. Along with the View menu options, you'll also find the Rotate Left and Rotate Right buttons and a Zoom percentage field—enter a number to zoom in or out to that view.

TIP
Booming and Zooming
To zoom in and out, switch to the **Zoom** tool and click in the image on the object on which you want to focus. To switch from zooming in to zooming out, click the **Minus** button in the options bar, then click the **Plus** button to switch back.

MAKING SHARPENING QUICK FIXES

When an image is just a bit out of focus, sometimes you can save it with a judicious application of sharpening. First, try the Sharpen Quick Fix's Auto button, which enables Photoshop Elements to determine automatically how much sharpening to apply. If you don't like the results, undo or click the **Cancel** button and try dragging the **Sharpen Amount** slider.

Start

1 Click

2 Click

3 Click and drag

1 With the picture you want to fix open in the Editor, click the **Quick** button at the top of the Palette Bin.

2 To have Photoshop Elements sharpen the image, click the **Auto Sharpen** button.

3 To adjust the amount of sharpening yourself, click and drag the **Amount** slider until the picture looks clear but not grainy.

End

TIP
Look Sharp
If you want more control over the sharpening procedure, choose **Enhance, Adjust Sharpness**. This command enables you to control the amount and intensity of sharpening very precisely.

CAUTION
Go Slowly
When you drag the Sharpen Amount slider to the right, you're increasing the amount of contrast between adjacent pixels in the image. Proceed with caution! If you sharpen the picture too much, it starts to look grainy.

CROPPING A PICTURE

One hallmark of a skilled photographer is pleasing composition, or arrangement of the things you're shooting within the picture frame. You can't always take the time to get the composition just right. Cropping used to be one of the most common fixes made in the darkroom—now you can do it with the lights on.

Start

End

1. With the picture you want to fix open in the Editor, click the **Quick** button at the top of the Palette Bin.

2. Choose the **Crop** tool from the toolbox, or press **C**.

3. With your picture open in the Editor, drag a corner of the cropping box to indicate the new framing.

4. Click the **Commit** button near the cropping marquee (or press **Enter** on the keyboard) to accept the change.

TIP

Adjusting Width and Height

After step 1, type a width and height in the options bar to match the proportions (type **5** for width and **7** for height for a 5 × 7 print). Or, press **Shift** while you drag to force a perfectly square selection.

TIP

Canceling the Crop

In step 3, to cancel the cropping operation, click the **Cancel** button (just left of the Commit button) near the cropping marquee or press **Esc**.

STRAIGHTENING A CROOKED PICTURE

Automatic straightening works best when the subject is just slightly out of alignment—a flagpole that appears to be leaning, for example. Photoshop Elements finds a strong vertical or horizontal line in the image and aligns the image by matching that line with the nearest 90° angle.

Start

2 Click

3 Click

1 Click

① With the picture open in the Editor, choose **Image**, **Rotate**, **Straighten Image**. Photoshop Elements aligns the image.

② Click the **Crop** tool in the toolbox, or press **C**.

③ Crop the photo to remove the white edges.

End

TIP
Severely Off-Angle?
If the subject is severely off-angle, use one of the **Image**, **Rotate** or **Image**, **Transform** commands instead; turn to Part 6, "Using Layers to Combine Photos and Artwork," for help.

TIP
Straighten *and* Crop
Photoshop Elements can both straighten *and* crop automatically (choose **Image**, **Rotate**, **Straighten and Crop Image**). But I've found the results to be rather sloppy. You'll be happier if you crop the image yourself.

ROTATING AN IMAGE ON OPENING

Like film cameras, digital cameras take all pictures in landscape orientation—with the long side of the frame horizontal. To take a portrait, you must physically rotate the camera. The most common reason to rotate an image in Photoshop Elements is so that you can view it correctly for editing and printing.

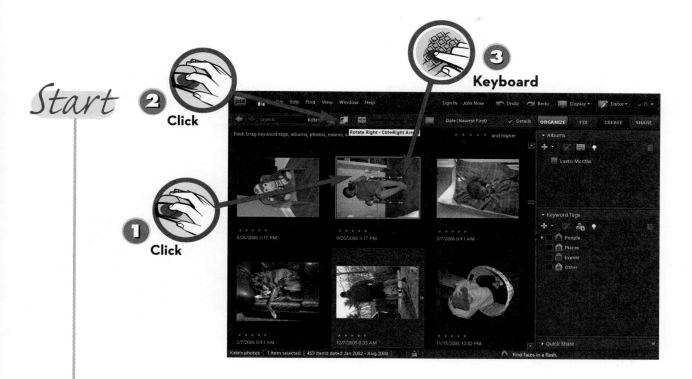

Start

2 Click

1 Click

3 Keyboard

1 In the Organizer, click the thumbnail of the picture you want to rotate.

2 Click the **Rotate Left** or the **Rotate Right** button in the options bar.

3 Press **Ctrl-I** to open the file for editing.

End

TIP

Quick and Easy Rotation

This method of rotating a picture has the same effect as choosing one of the Image, Rotate commands from the menu bar. But you'll find it's more convenient for quickly rotating all your portrait shots. If you click multiple thumbnails before you do step 2, you can apply the same rotation to multiple shots with a single command.

ROTATING AN IMAGE FOR ARTISTIC EFFECT

Graphic artists call this type of rotation a Dutch angle. Perhaps the most familiar example is the nightclub poster with rotated glamour portraits of the performers. It's a great technique for adding flair to greeting cards and family Web pages.

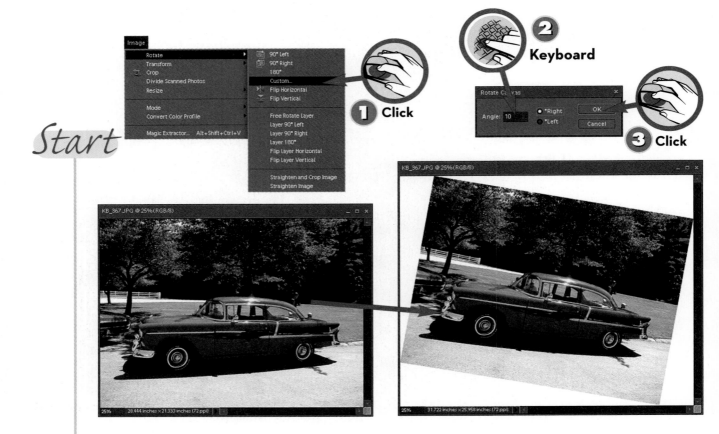

1. With the picture open in the Editor's Full Edit mode, choose **Image**, **Rotate**, **Custom**.

2. In the Rotate Canvas dialog, type a rotation angle in degrees (clockwise from 12 o'clock, or click **Left** for counterclockwise rotation).

3. Click **OK**.

Start

End

NOTE

Auto-Adjust Canvas Size

Photoshop Elements automatically increases the canvas size to create a frame large enough to hold the rotated picture without reducing the image size. The area outside the picture is the current background color.

TIP

Continuous Rotation

You can choose **Image**, **Rotate**, **Free Rotate Layer** and drag a corner to rotate the image continuously. However, this method doesn't increase canvas size, so the picture is cropped. If you apply this command to a background layer, Photoshop Elements asks if you want to convert it to a layer; click **OK**.

RESIZING AND RESAMPLING AN IMAGE

Digital photos are composed of a finite number of pixels. Resizing and resampling often go hand in hand: If you increase the size of an image, the result can look coarse unless you resample it to increase the resolution. If you reduce the image size, it decreases the resolution, resulting in a smaller file size.

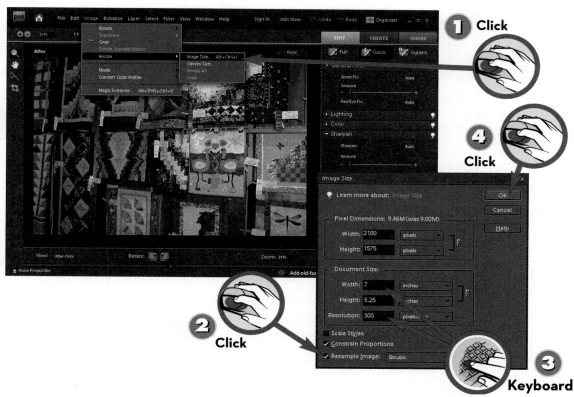

(1) With a picture open in the Editor, choose **Image**, **Resize**, **Image Size**.

(2) Click **Resample Image**.

(3) Type a new width in either Width field and a new value in the Resolution field.

(4) Click **OK**.

NOTE

Enter Width or Height

In step 3, enter width or height, but not both. If you enter one, the program calculates the other so that the image isn't distorted. The Resolution value should be 72 for email or the Web, 150–300 for making prints with a color inkjet printer.

TIP

Bicubic Is Best

For all but the slowest computers or very large images, leave the Resample Image option set to Bicubic, which gives the highest-quality result. Bilinear, which takes less processing time, is the next-best choice.

REMOVING A SCRATCH FROM AN IMAGE

Damage to old photos is a fact of life—but fortunately, it's one that's easy for Photoshop Elements to deal with. If your scanned photo shows rips or scratches—in this example, there seems to have been a light leak when the original print was developed—you can restore the parts of the image that have been obscured. You just have to take it slow and easy.

3 Click and drag

Start

① Click

② Alt-click

① With an image open in the Editor's Full Edit mode, choose the **Healing Brush** tool from the toolbox.

② Press **Alt** as you click a clear area that matches the area you want to fix.

③ Click and drag over the area you want to remove from the image.

End

NOTE
Know Your Tools
The Healing Brush works well for areas of relatively similar color and texture. If you need to fill in a more varied area, try using the Clone Stamp. Use several short strokes to blend the pixels in neatly.

NOTE
More Removal Magic
Turn to "Removing Blemishes," **p. 143**, to learn more about using the Healing Brush and its sibling, the Spot Healing Brush.

REMOVING RED EYE MANUALLY

The infamous red eye effect happens when the flash is mounted on or built in to the camera and the subject is looking directly into the lens. The retina of the eye bounces the light right back. Take these steps to dispel those smoldering looks.

1 Click

Start

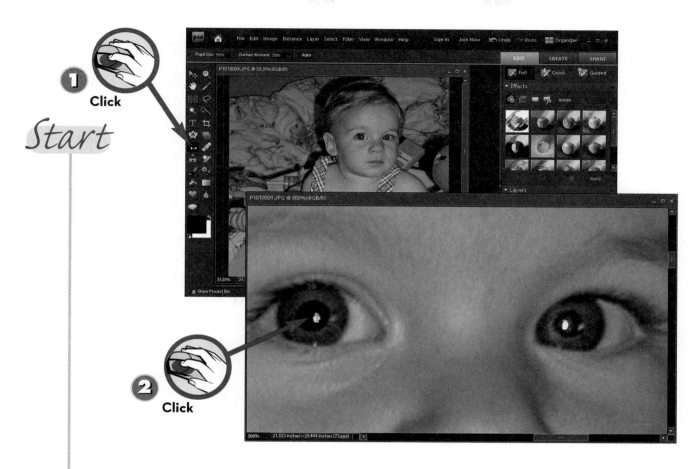

2 Click

1 With the photo that needs fixing open in the Editor's Full Edit mode, choose the **Red Eye Removal** tool, or press **Y**.

2 Click the red area in the photo to indicate the color you want to remove.

End

NOTE
Multicolored Reflections?
Remember that this command replaces only a single color. Red eye reflections may actually contain more than one shade of red. Repeat these steps for each individual color you need to remove.

TIP
Zooming Will Help
This task is much easier if you zoom in on the eye so that you can see the detail before you apply the brush. If the effect is tiny, you might be able to wash it out with a single click—no scrubbing. Switch to the Zoom tool to adjust the view.

ADVANCED PHOTO FIXING

Are you ready to kick it up a notch? Here's where your photo-editing skills become a bit more extensive. In this part, you'll learn how to brighten up dark photos, clarify blurry ones, make skin tones look more natural, and even change the color of Grandma's shirt if you like. Want to delete Cousin Steve's ex from the family portrait? No problem—just keep reading and you'll learn how to do that, too.

The first thing to learn, however, is how to isolate just the part of the image you want to work on to make sure you don't alter the rest of the picture unintentionally. The first three tasks in this part show you different ways to *select* part of an image so that you can work with it. Even if you skip the rest of the tasks in this part, don't skip these—creating selections is a skill you'll need over and over again.

As you learn these editing techniques, you'll realize why photographs are no longer considered proof of much of anything. Digital images are so easy to change that it's hard to know when you should stop. Try to use a light touch so that your photos still say the same things they did when you picked up your camera to shoot; the idea is just to make that message a bit clearer.

FOCUSING ON THE DETAILS

A dark, boring photo before...

...and a striking, colorful landscape after. You'll be amazed at what a few lighting and color adjustments and a bit of sharpening can accomplish.

USING GUIDED EDIT

If you believe you've moved beyond Quick Fix mode and are ready to try a few of the more advanced tools in Photoshop Elements, you might want to start with Guided Edit mode. In this mode, you use the same tools and controls as in Full Edit mode, but Photoshop Elements places them in the Palette Bin and walks you through their use step by step.

Start

① Click
② Click
③ Click
④ Click

1 With an image open in the Editor, click the **Guided** button to switch to Guided Edit mode.

2 In the list in the Palette Bin, click the task you want to complete.

3 Click the **View** button at the bottom of the Palette Bin to switch to the view mode you prefer.

4 Click **Tell Me More** to learn more about the task you're working on.

Continued

NOTE
Tools, More or Less
In Guided Edit mode, the toolbox contains even fewer tools than it does in Quick Fix mode. That's because Photoshop Elements puts the tools you need for each task right in the Palette Bin. If you want to use tools that aren't available, switch to Full Edit mode.

TIP
A View to an Edit
You'll best be able to gauge the effects of your settings if you switch to one of the Before & After modes in step 3. Use Before & After - Horizontal for vertically oriented pictures and Before & After - Vertical for horizontally oriented pictures.

5 Starting at the beginning, read and follow the instructions in the Palette Bin.

6 To undo the changes you've made and start over, click **Reset**.

7 When you've finished making edits, click **Done**.

End

TIP
Wait, There's More!
Some Guided Edit tasks have multiple steps and different options. Be sure you drag the scrollbar at the right side of the Palette Bin to display all the text in each Guided Edit task. And if you want to know more about the tools and techniques you're using in Guided Edit mode, click **Tell Me More** to see a Help page that explains everything.

SELECTING PART OF AN IMAGE

When you're painting the trim in your house, you use tape to mask off the parts of the wall where you don't want to get paint. That's what selections are all about in the Editor's Full Edit mode—with part of the image selected, any changes you make are applied to just that area, leaving the rest of the image untouched.

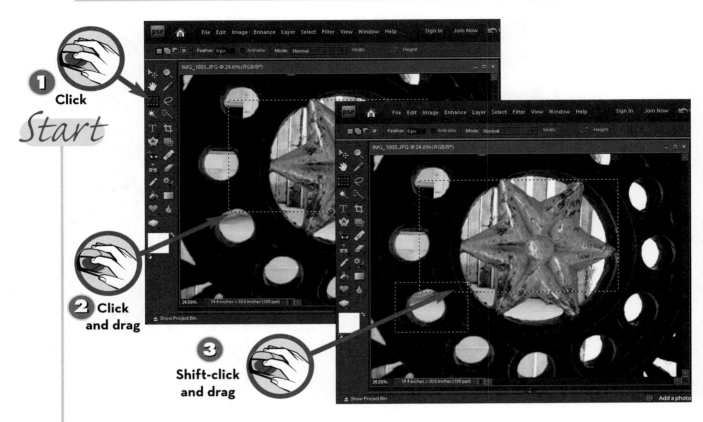

1 Click

Start

2 Click and drag

3 Shift-click and drag

1 With the Editor in Full Edit mode and an image open, click the **Rectangular Marquee** tool.

2 Click and drag to select a rectangular portion of the image.

3 Shift-click and drag to add to the selection marquee.

Continued

TIP

Circles and Squares

When drawing selections using one of the marquee tools—the Rectangular Marquee or the Elliptical Marquee—you can create squares or circles, respectively, by pressing **Shift** as you drag out the selection.

NOTE

Shift This, Shift That

When you want to add to an existing selection, be sure to press **Shift** *before* you click in the image to draw the next part of the selection. If you click outside the selection without Shift or Alt held down, the existing selection disappears.

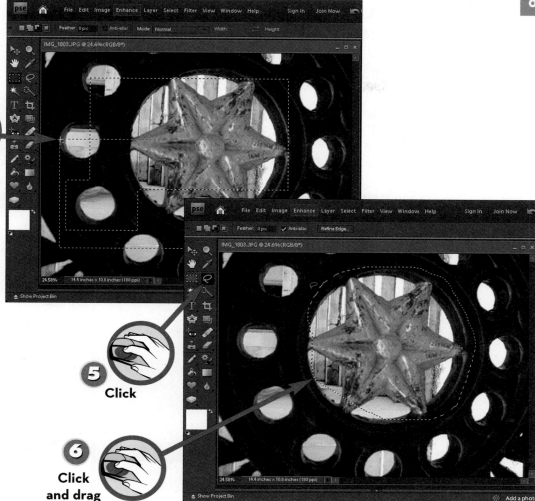

4 Alt-click and drag

5 Click

6 Click and drag

4 Alt-click and drag to remove part of the selection marquee.

5 Click the **Lasso** tool.

6 Click and drag around any part of the image to select an irregular area.

End

NOTE
Mix It Up
You can use any combination of selection tools to create a selection that's just the shape you're looking for. For example, you might start out with a rectangular or circular selection, then use the Lasso tool to add and subtract smaller areas.

TIP
Selection Magnetism
Click and hold the **Lasso** tool to display the Magnetic Lasso. To create a selection with it, click in the image, and then click again to indicate a corner point of the selection area. Close the selection by clicking the first point again.

MAKING SELECTIONS MAGICALLY

You might have thought the Magic Wand was enough magic for one program—but you haven't seen the Quick Selection Brush yet! With this funky tool, you scribble across the area you want to select, and Elements figures out what you want selected.

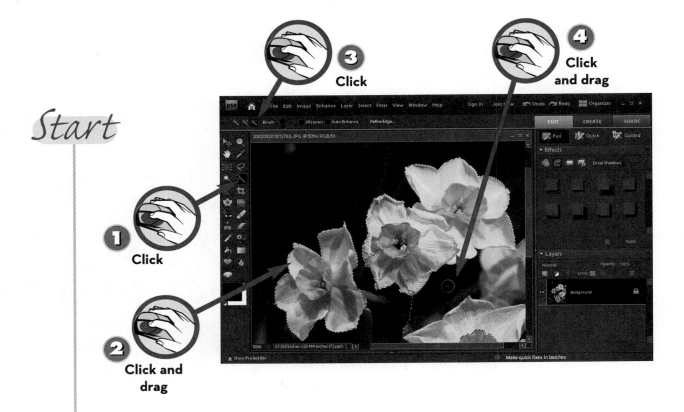

Start

End

1. With the Editor in Full Edit mode and an image open, click the **Quick Selection Brush** tool.

2. With the Quick Selection Brush tool, click and drag to roughly cover the area you want to select.

3. Click the **Subtract from Selection** button on the options bar.

4. Click and drag to remove areas from your selection.

TIP

The Magic Modes

Three buttons on the options bar control the behavior of the Quick Selection Brush. You always start in New Selection mode, and you can click this button at any time to start your selection over. Click **Add to Selection** when you want to paint over more colors that should be included in the selection—Elements automatically switches to this mode after you make your initial strokes with the tool. Finally, click **Subtract from Selection** when you want to paint over areas that should *not* be included in the selection.

SELECTING AREAS BASED ON COLOR

With the Magic Wand tool, you can quickly select an irregular area that's all the same color, such as a flower, a T-shirt, or even the sky. By changing the Tolerance value, you can make the Magic Wand more or less picky about how closely a color must match your target color to be selected.

Start

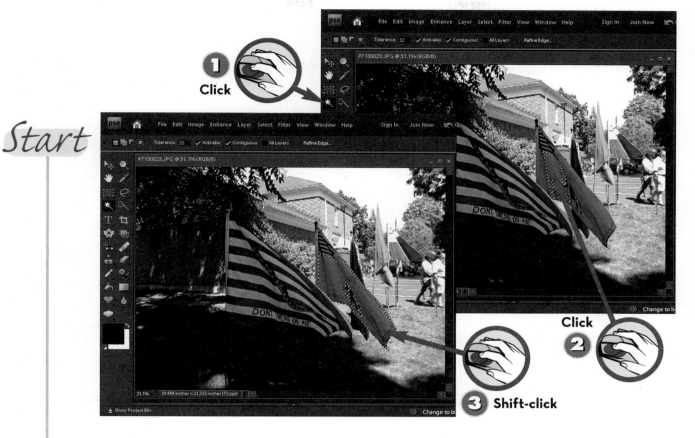

Click ❶

Click ❷

❸ **Shift-click**

❶ With the Editor in Full Edit mode and an image open, click the **Magic Wand** tool.

❷ Click a solid-colored area of the photo to select it.

❸ Shift-click another spot to add another area to the selection.

End

TIP
All About Tolerance
Tolerance can range from 0 to 255, and it determines how close a pixel's color must be to the pixel you click to be included in the selection. At 0, only pixels that match the original pixel exactly will be selected; at 255, the entire picture will be selected.

TIP
Right Next Door
When the Contiguous box on the options bar is checked, the Magic Wand selects only those pixels that are next to each other in the image. To select pixels of the same color throughout the image, uncheck **Contiguous**.

REFINING A SELECTION

Often, a selection made with the Magic Wand or the Quick Selection tool has ragged edges or includes a "halo" around the object you were trying to select. Fixing these problems is simple, using the Refine Edge dialog.

1 Click and drag

Start

2 Click

4 Click

3 Drag

1 With the Editor in Full Edit mode and an image open, make a selection using any selection tool.

2 Choose **Select**, **Refine Edge**.

3 Drag the sliders to smooth, blur, or resize the selection.

4 Click **OK**.

End

NOTE
In the Mode
The Refine Edge dialog can use two different preview modes: Standard Selection mode, which shows you "marching ants" around the selection's edges, or Overlay mode, which gives you a better idea of the selection's shape, particularly if you're feathering it.

NOTE
Handy Zooming
Use the Zoom and Hand tools in the Refine Edge dialog to take a closer look at selection edges while you're adjusting your settings. Using these tools doesn't affect the active tool in the main toolbox.

BRIGHTENING UP SHADOWED AREAS

If you're like many users of Photoshop Elements, the Shadows/Highlights command may turn out to be the one that you use on nearly every photo. It's not considered a Quick Fix—yet its results are amazing and you'll love its ease of use.

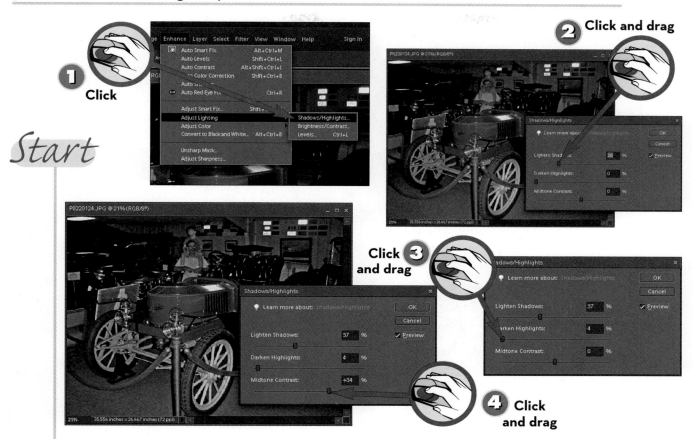

Start

End

1. With the Editor in Full Edit mode and an image open, choose **Enhance**, **Adjust Lighting**, **Shadows/Highlights**.

2. Click and drag the **Lighten Shadows** slider to the right to bring out shadow detail.

3. Click and drag the **Darken Highlights** slider to the right to tone down the image's bright areas.

4. Click and drag the **Midtone Contrast** slider to the right to make the image's colors stand out more against a dark background.

CAUTION
Easy Does It
Be careful not to increase shadow lightness too much—it's fun to bring out the shadow details that you didn't even realize were there, but shadows that are too light don't contrast enough with the brighter areas of an image.

NOTE
The Starting Point
Elements always starts you out with a 25% increase in shadow lightness. For most images taken with a point-and-shoot camera, especially indoor shots, that provides an amazing improvement. Adjust the percentage up or down until you're happy with the picture.

CORRECTING A COLOR CAST

If a photo has an undesirable overall tint, it's because the image's *white balance* is off. Daylight has a blue cast, light bulbs indoors make everything orange, and fluorescents can make faces a sickly green. This command compensates by rebalancing all the colors in the picture in relation to pure white.

Start

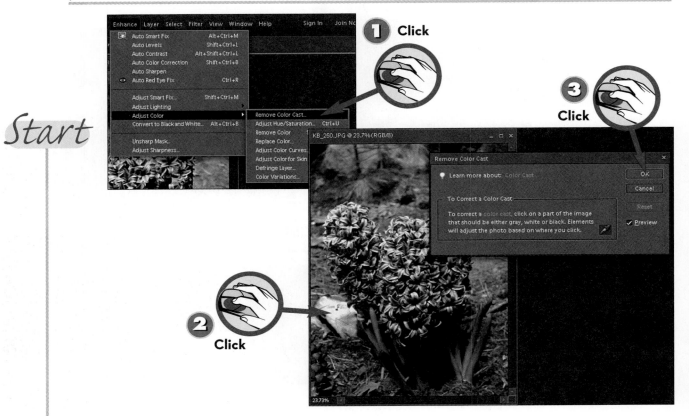

1. With the Editor in Full Edit mode and an image open, choose **Enhance**, **Adjust Color**, **Remove Color Cast**.

2. Click an area of the image that should be white.

3. Click **OK**.

End

TIP

Pick Pure White

In step 2, pick an area such as teeth, the white of an eye, or a white tablecloth or shirt collar. Any blown-out (overexposed) area usually gives the best result. If there's no white anywhere in the picture, click a neutral area (gray or black).

ADJUSTING SKIN TONES

This is a handy command designed specifically to fix "off" skin tones in photos of people. You can compensate for poor lighting by lightening or darkening skin tones and changing the picture's yellow/pink balance. You can also adjust overall lighting of the scene.

Start

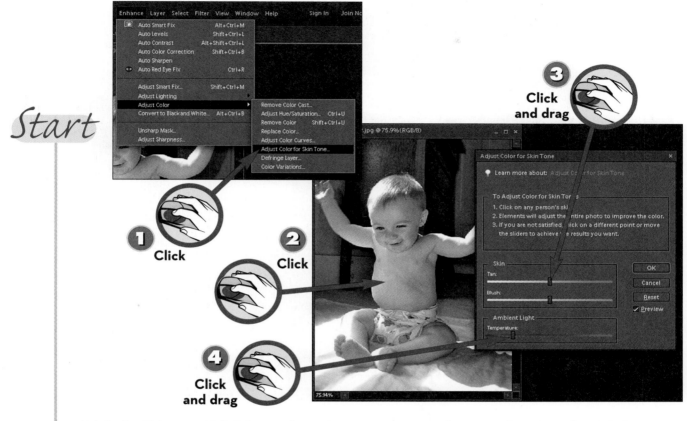

3 Click and drag

1 Click

2 Click

4 Click and drag

1. With the Editor in Full Edit mode and an image open, choose **Enhance**, **Adjust Color**, **Adjust Color for Skin Tone**.

2. Click a patch of skin in the image. Elements adjusts all the skin tones in that range within the picture.

3. To refine the skin tones, click and drag the **Tan** and **Blush** sliders.

4. Click and drag the **Temperature** slider to make the entire image look warmer or cooler.

End

NOTE

Tone Deaf

Elements looks at the color of the area you click to determine which colors in a photo qualify as skin tones. If people in your photo have widely varying skin colors, you might not find this command as useful as it is when the subjects' skin colors are similar.

EXPLORING COLOR VARIATIONS

Perhaps it's not that the colors in the picture are wrong, you just want them to be different. For example, an interior decorator might want to view a room in a different light or with the decor a different shade. Experiment with color variations, which can be more dramatic than just correcting the picture's overall cast.

Start

1 Click

2 Click

3 Click and drag

1. With the Editor in Full Edit mode and an image open, choose **Enhance**, **Adjust Color**, **Color Variations**.

2. Click a radio button to choose what part of the image you want to adjust.

3. Click and drag the **Amount** slider to make the differences between the Variation thumbnails greater or less.

Continued

TIP
Adjust Midtones First
Adjusting midtones (values ranging between shadows and highlights) usually give you more noticeable results than working with shadows, highlights, or saturation. To change the magnitude of an effect, drag the **Adjust Color Intensity** slider before you apply it.

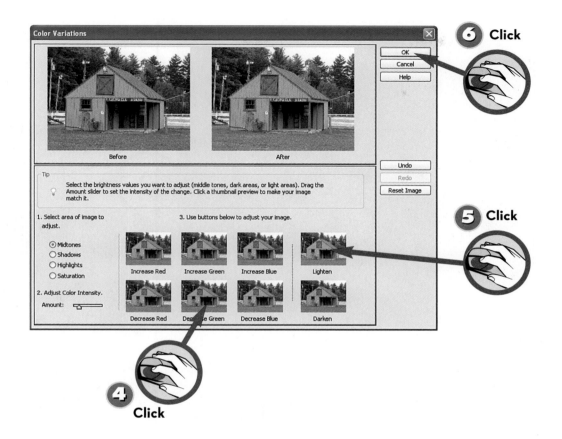

4 Click a thumbnail, such as Decrease Green, to change color or brightness in the shot.

5 Click the same thumbnail again to increase its effect, or click another thumbnail to adjust a different color, or the image's brightness.

6 When the After image looks right, click **OK**.

End

TIP

Take Baby Steps

The default setting for Adjust Color Intensity is usually a bit too powerful, meaning that it changes the image too much with each click. It's better to drag the slider to the left and then click multiple times on a thumbnail, building up an effect gradually, than to click once with a higher intensity setting and end up changing the image too much.

REPLACING A SPECIFIC COLOR

Don't like the color of that dress? Does the sofa clash with the drapes? Want to make the sky pink or the river run green? You can make it so at no extra charge—with your choices limited only by your design sense.

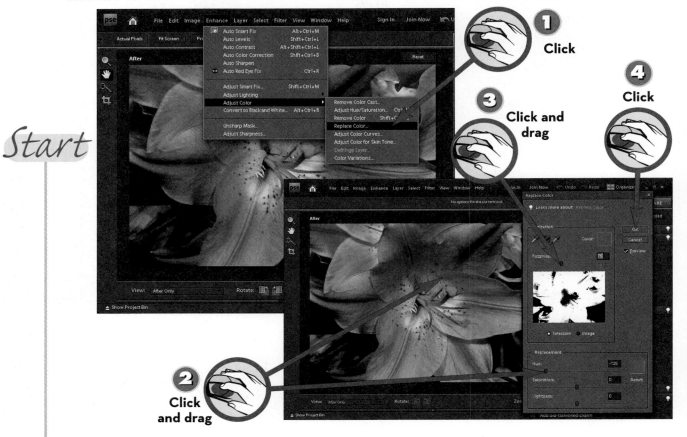

Start

End

1. With the Editor in Full Edit mode and an image open, choose **Enhance**, **Adjust Color**, **Replace Color**.

2. Click within an area in the picture; then click and drag the **Replacement** sliders until you see the color you want in the Sample box.

3. Click and drag the **Fuzziness** slider to adjust the selection by changing the number of related shades that it includes.

4. Click **OK**.

TIP

Add or Subtract
Click the **Add to Sample** or **Subtract from Sample** eyedroppers (marked with + and -) and click the area in the picture to add or remove it. Then, dragging the **Replacement** sliders applies the color change to the entire selection.

NOTE

What Changes?
These steps change all instances of the same color anywhere in the image, not just on the area you select in step 2.

ADJUSTING BRIGHTNESS AND CONTRAST

Sometimes a Quick Fix like Auto Contrast just doesn't do the trick—especially if the image has bright highlights, deep shadows, or both. These steps give you more control so that you can make continuous adjustments while previewing the result.

Start

Click ①

Click ③

Click and drag ②

① With the Editor in Full Edit mode and an image open, choose **Enhance**, **Adjust Lighting**, **Brightness/Contrast**.

② Click and drag one or both sliders, **Brightness** or **Contrast**, until the picture looks right.

③ Click **OK**.

End

NOTE

Overall Change

Changing brightness and contrast affects the entire image unless you select a particular area first. Some of the available selection tools are Rectangular Marquee (for rectangular areas), Lasso (for irregular areas), and Magic Wand (for intricate shapes).

TIP

Subject in the Dark?

If your subject is too dark overall (underexposed), try choosing **Enhance**, **Adjust Lighting**, **Shadows/Highlights** first. It boosts brightness only in the darker areas, leaving the lighter areas—usually, the background—alone.

CHANGING A COLOR PHOTO TO BLACK AND WHITE

You'll occasionally need black-and-white pictures for newsletters that will be printed in one color—or perhaps when you're in a vintage-movie kind of mood. You can easily convert your color shots to black and white, but don't forget to adjust the contrast before clicking OK, to make them suitably snappy.

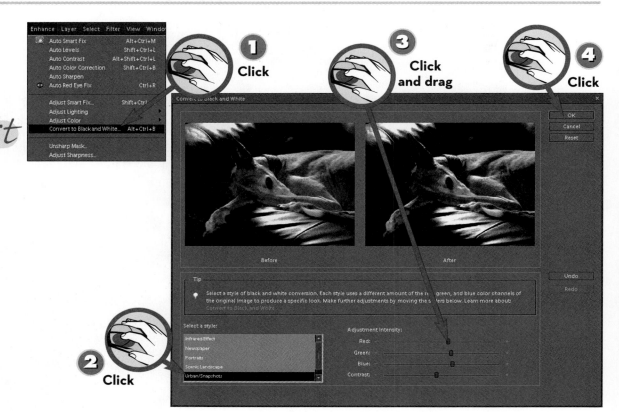

Start

1 Click

3 Click and drag

4 Click

2 Click

1 With the Editor in Full Edit mode and an image open, choose **Enhance**, **Convert to Black and White** or press **Ctrl+Alt+B**.

2 Choose an appropriate style for the image.

3 Click and drag the **Adjustment Intensity** sliders to refine the conversion.

4 Click **OK**.

End

TIP
Brown Study
Sepia (a brownish monochrome) is actually a color effect. After converting to black and white and adjusting contrast, choose **Image**, **Mode**, **RGB Color**; then apply one or more Color Variations to colorize the image.

REMOVING OBJECTS FROM AN IMAGE

To take a great photo, you have to catch both the subject and the setting at just the right time. In case another object intrudes into the scene at the crucial second, Photoshop Elements makes it easy to remove that little "extra" at a later date.

Start

2 Alt-click

1 Click

3 Click and drag

 1 With the Editor in Full Edit mode and an image open, click the **Clone Stamp** tool or press **S**.

2 Press **Alt** as you click a clear area that matches the background.

3 Click and drag over the object you want to remove from the image.

End

NOTE
Take Your Time
You might need to apply the Clone Stamp multiple times, using short strokes, to blend the new pixels in with the existing background.

NOTE
Object Removal Magic
The Clone Stamp tool is a good choice for removing objects on irregular backgrounds and for larger objects. For small objects, Elements includes special "healing" tools. Turn to "Removing Blemishes," **p. 143**, to learn more.

REMOVING UNWANTED OBJECTS AUTOMATICALLY

Does this ever happen to you? You think you've got the perfect shot, but then you get home, offload the pictures on your camera, and find that your perfect shot actually has an obnoxious pigeon in the foreground that you didn't notice at the time. Well, as long as you have a backup shot or two of the same scene, Photoshop Elements can get rid of that pigeon in about two seconds flat.

Start

1 In the Organizer, select all the shots of the scene that you want to clean up.

2 Choose **File**, **New**, **Photomerge Scene Cleaner**. The images open in the Editor, with instructions in the Palette Bin.

3 In the Project Bin, choose the best shot and drag it to the Final preview.

4 Click another photo in the Project Bin to display it as the Source image.

Continued

 NOTE
Final Step: Crop
After you've created the final composite image, you'll usually need to crop it to remove white areas around the edges. These exist because Photoshop Elements makes room for everything shown in all the selected images.

 TIP
Matching Up
Scene Cleaner works only with photos that are very similar. So when you're shooting a scene, try to keep your camera at the same distance from it and pointed in the same direction.

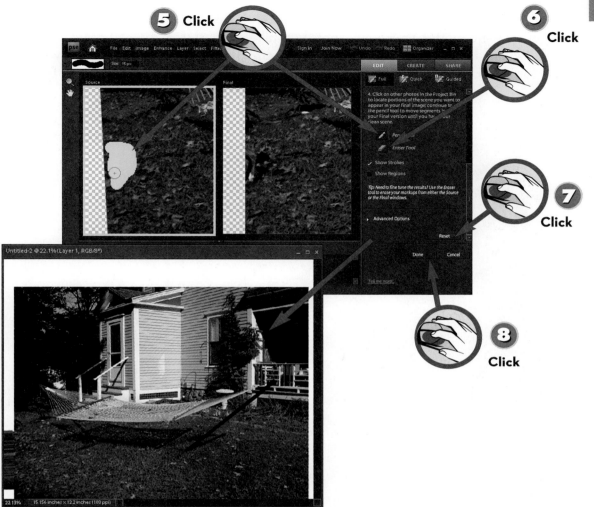

5 Click the **Pencil** tool and draw over areas in the Source image that you want to merge into the Final photo. (I'm replacing my dog's hind leg with grass.)

6 To remove areas from the Final photo, click the **Eraser** tool and erase the Pencil marks.

7 Click **Reset** if you want to start over.

8 Click **Done** when the Final preview looks the way you want it to.

End

NOTE

Facing the Truth?

When you chose Photomerge Scene Cleaner from the New submenu, you may have noticed another command called Photomerge Faces. Photoshop Elements can do a fun party trick: Combine facial features from different pictures to produce an "if A and B had a kid" picture that shares elements of both pictures. Give it a try!

COMBINING THE BEST FROM MULTIPLE PHOTOS

It never fails—no matter how many shots you take of everyone at a gathering, *someone's* always looking the wrong way, or blinking, or scratching an itch. Fortunately, if you save all those funky shots, Photoshop Elements can help you merge them into one perfect picture.

Start

1. In the Organizer, select all the pictures that you want to combine.

2. Choose **File**, **New**, **Photomerge Group Shot**. The images open in the Editor, with instructions in the Palette Bin.

3. In the Project Bin, choose the best group shot and drag it to the Final preview.

4. Click another photo in the Project Bin to display it as the Source image.

Continued

NOTE

Show Me

You can control how Photoshop Elements indicates the areas that are being copied from the Source image to the Final image. Click **Show Strokes** to show your Pencil strokes in the source image (this setting is on by default), and click **Show Regions** to reveal the copied areas in the Final image. Turn off these settings to see how the Final image will appear after you have finished.

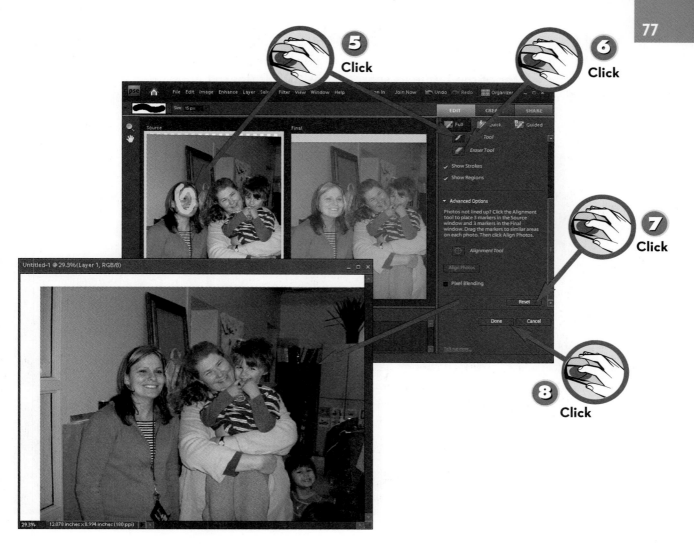

5 Click the **Pencil** tool and draw over areas in the Source image that you want to merge into the Final photo.

6 To remove areas from the final photo, click the **Eraser** tool and erase the Pencil marks.

7 Click **Reset** if you want to start over.

8 Click **Done** when the Final preview looks the way you want it to.

End

TIP

Toeing the Line

If the photos aren't lined up correctly in the Final image preview, click the **Alignment** tool, click to place three markers in the Source image and three markers at the corresponding points in the Final image, and then click **Align Photos**.

NOTE

Color Coding

The Source photos in the Project Bin are color coded so that you can keep track of which one is supplying which areas in the Final image. If you click the Show Regions box in the Palette Bin, Photoshop Elements highlights the parts of the Final image from each Source image.

SHARPENING A BLURRY PHOTO

Digital cameras have an *auto-focus* feature, which attempts to make the edges of the subject in the center of the frame as sharp as possible. It doesn't always work. For more consistent results, learn how to focus manually. But, you can always try this simple technique to sharpen slightly blurred shots.

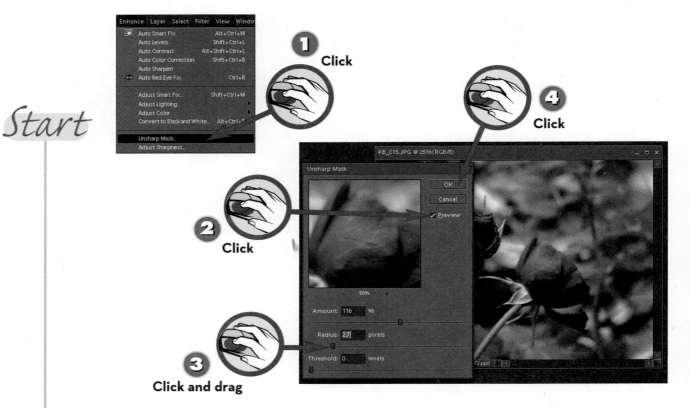

Start

Click

Click

Click

Click and drag

End

1 With the Editor in Full Edit mode and an image open, choose **Enhance**, **Unsharp Mask**.

2 Click the **Preview** check box to see your changes in the image window.

3 Click and drag the sliders to sharpen the image.

4 Click **OK** when you're happy with the picture.

NOTE

Focus Manually

Sharpening an image can improve the look of a blurred shot somewhat, but it's no substitute for proper manual focusing. That's particularly true when you're doing *close-ups*—with the subject fewer than four feet away.

TIP

Don't Overdo It

If the picture starts to look too sharp, drag the **Threshold** slider to the right to limit the areas to which the sharpening is applied, and then lower the **Amount** percentage.

MAKING EDGES SOFTER

There are at least two good reasons to soften focus: It can make a portrait look more flattering, blending out lines, pores, and small blemishes; and it can save a shot that's only slightly out of focus—making the softness look more deliberate.

Start

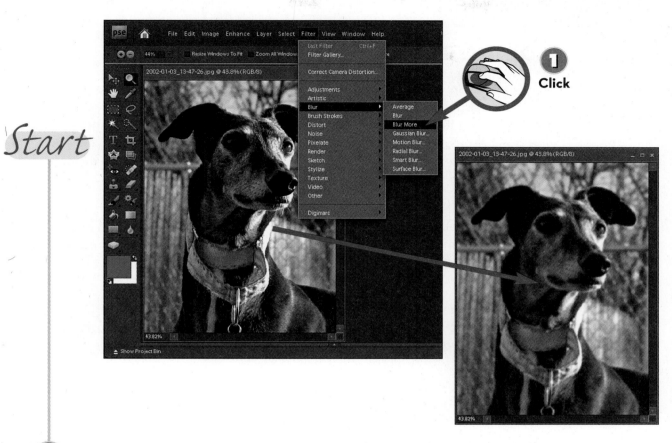

1 Click

1 With the Editor in Full Edit mode and an image open, choose **Filter**, **Blur**, **Blur More**.

End

 TIP
An Artful Blur
This task uses Blur More because the result of the Blur command can be hard to see. The other Blur commands in the Blur submenu are for when you're feeling arty.

5

ADDING TITLES AND TEXT

Printing text on your photos can turn your digital snapshots into greeting cards, invitations, postcards, or posters. An interesting photo with a caption can be a news item for a community newsletter or family Website. And, even if you don't aspire to craft your own greetings or write your own news, including captions in your picture files is a much better way of identifying and describing your photos than writing on the back of the prints.

As you gain skill working with text, you'll want the flexibility of keeping different pieces of text on separate *layers*, which work like clear sheets of plastic you can draw on. Layers permit you to add text and artwork without making any permanent changes to the underlying image. So be sure to take a look at the tasks in Part 6, "Using Layers to Combine Photos and Artwork."

Don't worry; none of this is complicated. Photoshop Element's built-in features help you create professional-looking output, whether it be for a Website or picture postcard, without having to sweat the technical details.

SAY IT WITH PICTURES AND WORDS

Adding a caption can give a photo "news value."

Don's new Kawasaki motorcycle is much redder than his previous Yamaha model.

Why not think of your life as a game—and you're the star!

ADDING AND PRINTING PHOTO CAPTIONS

This method of adding a caption to a photo stores the text information with the image file. When you check the Caption check box in the Print Preview dialog box, your photo prints with the caption outside the image area, centered beneath it.

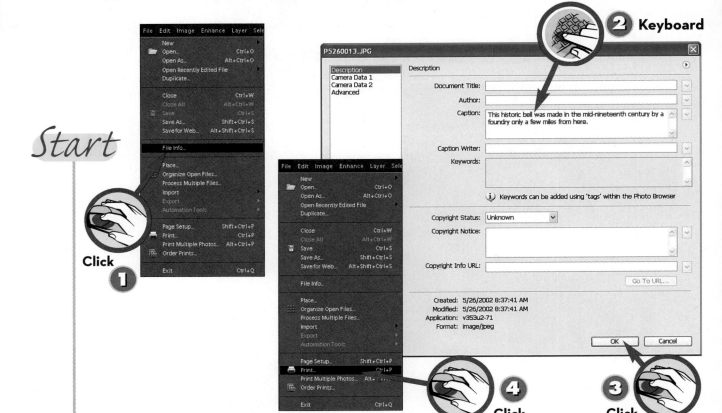

Start

1. With the Editor in Full Edit mode and an image open, choose **File**, **File Info**.

2. Type a descriptive caption in the Caption text field.

3. Click **OK**.

4. Choose **File**, **Print**.

Continued

NOTE
Dear Diary...
In step 2, the Caption text field can hold about 25 double-spaced pages. That's enough to paste a whole text document from the Clipboard. You could use it to hold your journal entries from a trip, for example.

NOTE
Title and Author Boxes
You can also type entries into the Document Title and Author boxes seen on the File Info dialog. However, only the Caption field is printed by this procedure.

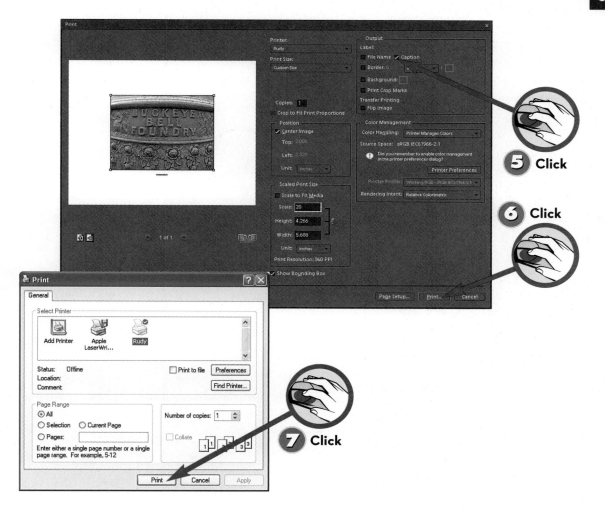

 5 Check the **Caption** check box.

6 Click **Print**.

7 Click **Print** in the Print dialog box.

End

TIP

Fitting on the Page

If you haven't sized the image to fit the canvas and the canvas to the paper size, choose **Fit on Page** from the Print Size pop-up menu in the Print Preview dialog box. Photoshop Elements will fit to the paper size chosen for the printer.

OVERLAYING TYPE ON AN IMAGE

Here's the direct approach—just type over an image anywhere you want. You can press Enter between typing multiple lines in the same block of text, or you can click the Commit button, and then repeat these steps to create a separate block that you can move and work with independently.

Start

End

1 With the Editor in Full Edit mode and an image open, choose the **Horizontal Type** tool.

2 Click the position in the image where you want the text to begin.

3 Type a line of text. To start a second line, press **Enter** and keep typing.

NOTE
Alignment Options
The starting point for the text line in step 2 depends on the current Alignment setting in the options bar (Left Align, Centered, or Right Align).

NOTE
New Text Layer
These steps create a new text layer automatically. Think of a layer as a clear sheet you can write or draw on without changing the image underneath.

ADDING PARAGRAPH TYPE

In addition to point text (click and type), Photoshop Elements enables you to create paragraph text. This text stays within the bounding box you specify, wrapping to the next line whenever it hits the right margin. In every other way, paragraph text is just like point text, and you can edit it the same way.

1 Click

2 Click and drag

4 Click and drag

3 Keyboard

Start

1 Switch to the **Horizontal Type** tool.

2 Click and drag in the photo to define the area you want the type to occupy.

3 Enter your text.

4 With the Type tool still active, click and drag a corner handle to reshape the type's bounding box.

End

NOTE

When and Why

Use paragraph text when you're adding more than just a few words of text and when the precise place where each new line begins isn't important to you.

TIP

Selective Selecting

When you're editing text, double-click to select a whole word. Triple-click to select an entire line, and quadruple-click to select a paragraph. Finally, quintuple-click (wow!) to select the entire contents of a text block.

SELECTING AND EDITING TYPE

Before you can edit text, you must first highlight the letters you want to replace. This works just the same way it does in your favorite word processor: Click and drag across the text you want to select.

Start

① Click

② Click and drag

③ Keyboard

End

④ Click

① Choose the **Horizontal Type** tool.

② Click and drag over the characters you want to replace.

③ Type the replacement characters.

④ Click the **Commit** button in the options bar.

TIP
Inserting Characters
To add one or more characters to your text, rather than replace some, click at the insertion point in step 2 and type.

NOTE
Keep Text Editable
You can't edit text after the text layers have been merged with the image (as in a JPEG file, for example). To keep text editable, save your work as a native Photoshop file (PSD).

CHANGING FONTS AND TYPE PROPERTIES

Words or even individual characters can have different properties, such as color or font, than adjacent characters in the same block.

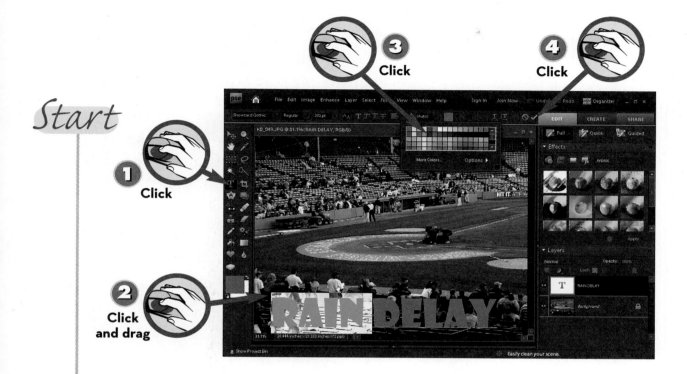

Start

End

1. Choose the **Horizontal Type** tool.

2. Click and drag over the characters you want to change.

3. Choose new text properties from the pop-up menus in the options bar, such as Color.

4. Click the **Commit** button in the options bar.

NOTE

Text Properties

Settings for all text properties become available in the options bar when a text object is selected in the Editor.

TIP

Lines and Blocks of Text

Create the text in a single text block rather than individual ones when you want Photoshop Elements to take care of alignment and spacing between lines.

ADDING A TALK BUBBLE

Oh, those wacky relatives and the wild things they say! A *talk bubble* can add a whimsical touch to your greeting cards and email. It's actually just one of many shapes that Photoshop Elements can draw so that you don't have to create them freehand.

Start

1 **Right-click**

2 **Click**

3 **Click**

4 **Click and drag**

1 Right-click the **Rectangle** tool.

2 Choose the **Custom Shape** tool.

3 Choose the talk bubble shape in the options bar and set the **Color** pop-up menu to **White**.

4 Click and drag to resize the shape in the image area.

Continued

-TIP-
Hearts and Flowers
The talk bubble—or *speech balloon*—is just one of an assortment of custom shapes. To pick one, after choosing the Custom Shape tool, choose the **Shape** pop-up menu in the options bar.

-NOTE-
Oh, By the Way
After you create the talk bubble and the text, you'll need to resize and position the text to fit correctly within the bounds of the bubble.

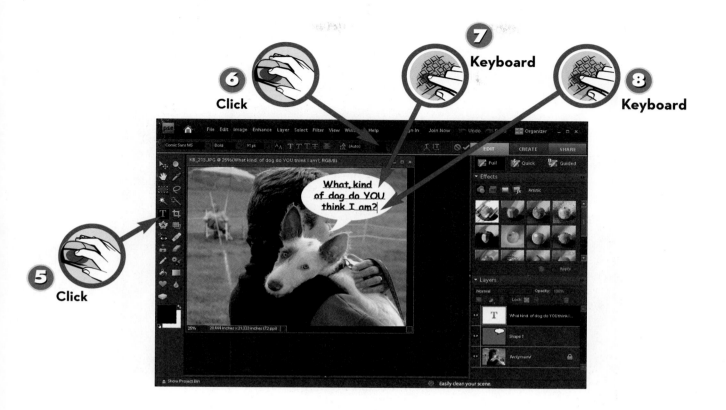

5 Choose the **Horizontal Type** tool.

6 Choose a color from the Color pop-up menu in the options bar.

7 Click inside the talk bubble and type some text.

8 Press **Enter** on the numeric keypad when you have finished typing the text.

End

TIP

Don't See a Talk Bubble?

The toolbar shows the Custom Shape tool you used last. If the talk bubble isn't there, choose the **Custom Shape** tool and choose the shape you want from the **Shape** box in the options bar.

NOTE

Other Shape Tools

Besides custom shapes, other tools in the Shape submenu in the toolbar are Rectangle, Rounded Rectangle, Ellipse, Polygon, and Line.

APPLYING A TYPE EFFECT

You can apply layer styles in the Effects palette to a selected type layer with a simple double-click. If Photoshop Elements didn't include these "canned" effects, you'd have to be a skilled graphic artist (and it would take a lot more work) to reproduce them.

1 Choose the **Move** tool, or press **V**.

2 Click the text that needs the effect. (**Auto Select Layer** must be checked.)

3 In the Effects palette, click the **Layer Styles** button, and then choose **Show All** from the rightmost menu.

4 Double-click the effect you want, such as Salt.

TIP

Effects Palette Open?
To clear your work area, you might want to close or dock the Effects palette when you're finished. If it's not in the Palette Bin, you can always get it back by choosing **Window, Effects**.

NOTE

Applying Text Effects
You'll also find a range of neat text effects in the Content palette (choose **Window, Content**). Choose **By Type** from the first pop-up menu at the top of the palette, and then choose **Text** from the second menu. Double-click a thumbnail to apply that effect to the selected layer.

ADDING A DROP SHADOW TO TYPE

Place a drop shadow behind text to make it appear to "pop" out from the background so that it's more readable. This is particularly handy when the background has both light and dark areas and you can't find a solid area to serve as a background for the text that gives enough contrast.

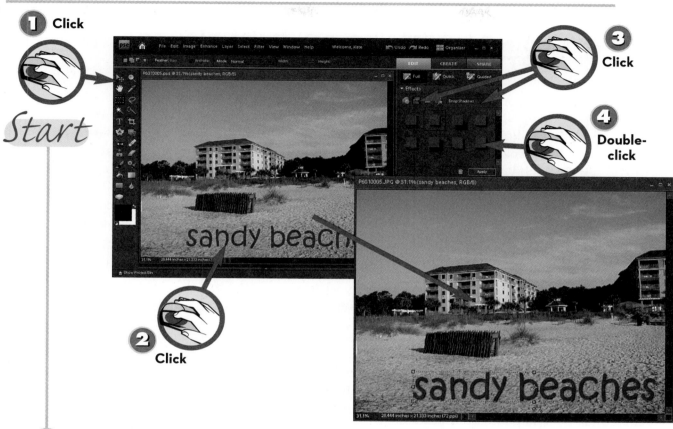

1. Choose the **Move** tool, or press **V**.

2. Click the text to which the drop shadow will be added. (**Auto Select Layer** must be checked.)

3. Click the Effects palette's **Layer Styles** button, and then choose **Drop Shadows** from the pop-up menu.

4. Double-click the drop shadow effect you want, such as **Hard Edge**.

End

NOTE
Auto Select Layer
For step 2 to work, the **Auto Select Layer** box must be checked in the options bar (the usual setting). If it's not checked, you must switch to the corresponding type layer using the Layers palette.

NOTE
Make Your Own?
You can experiment with creating your own drop-shadow effects if you know this: A drop shadow is actually a duplicate of the text object, in a contrasting color, positioned behind it at a slight offset, and usually blurred.

6

USING LAYERS TO COMBINE PHOTOS AND ARTWORK

If you know how animated movies were made in the days before computer generation, you're already familiar with the concept of layers. Animation artists traditionally used a process called ink-and-paint to draw cartoon characters on transparent sheets of celluloid, or cels. One new cel had to be created for each time a character moved. Cels were then placed over elaborately painted backgrounds, such as witches' castles or the decks of pirate ships. Painting on separate layers—the animated character on the cel and the background beneath—made it possible to reuse the same background throughout a long scene.

Layers in Photoshop Elements work much the same way. The image you begin with is the Background layer. Every layer you add starts out as transparent until you change its color, change its adjustment properties, or add objects to it.

If you've done any of the tasks in other parts involving shapes or text, you were working with layers, whether you realized it or not. Understand that building more complex layered images isn't for beginners. But, you should learn some of this if you want to graduate to more ambitious tasks.

The postcard on the facing page is actually built from 10 layers, including the background. Photoshop Elements permits as many as 8,000 layers—provided you don't run out of computer memory first!

A TEN-LAYERED IMAGE

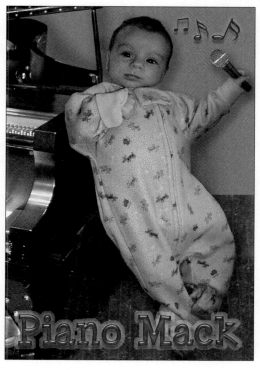

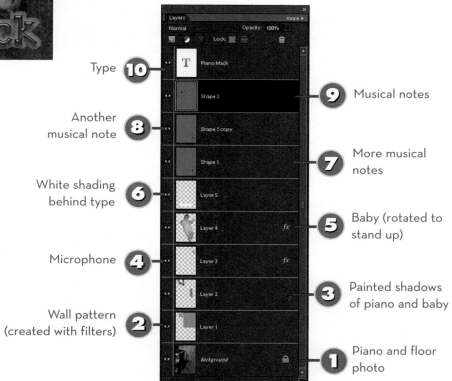

Type — 10 — Piano Mack

9 — Musical notes (Shape 2)

Another musical note — 8 — Shape 1 copy

7 — More musical notes (Shape 1)

White shading behind type — 6 — Layer 5

5 — Baby (rotated to stand up) (Layer 4)

Microphone — 4 — Layer 3

3 — Painted shadows of piano and baby (Layer 2)

Wall pattern (created with filters) — 2 — Layer 1

1 — Piano and floor photo (Background)

PAINTING ON A NEW LAYER

A new layer is created for you automatically whenever you use the Shape or Type tools—also, whenever you paste (choose **Edit**, **Paste**) or choose certain other commands on the Layers menu. If you work with any other tools, you should create a new layer for painting, drawing, or adding new shapes to your photo.

Start

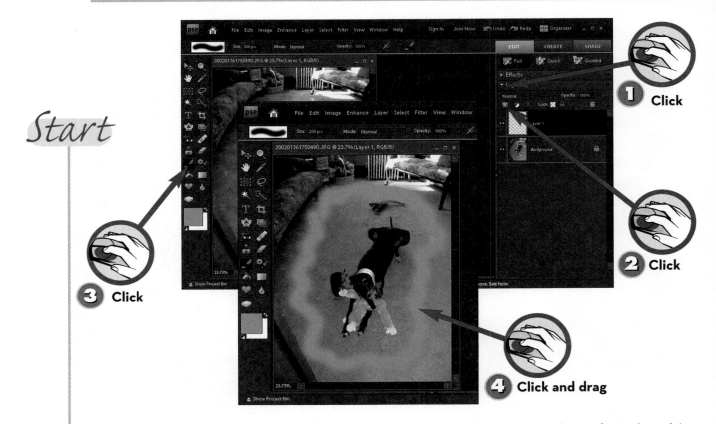

③ **Click**

① **Click**

② **Click**

④ **Click and drag**

① With an image open in the Editor's Full Edit mode, open the Layers palette if it's closed (or choose **Window**, **Layers** if you don't see it in the Palette Bin).

② Click the **Create a New Layer** button (or choose **Layer**, **New**, **Layer**).

③ Choose a tool, such as the Brush.

④ Paint on the layer.

End

TIP
Simplify and Merge
Simplifying changes vector shapes and text (based on geometry) to pixels—editable as dots, not as shapes. Merging both simplifies the active (selected) layer and combines it with the layer beneath. You can't manipulate text and shapes individually after merging. If you see a warning that the layer must be simplified before proceeding with a tool, choose **Cancel** and create a new layer using these steps; then switch back to the tool and paint or draw.

COPYING AN OBJECT TO A NEW LAYER

Selecting an object on the Background layer, making changes, and then saving your work changes the original image forever. Instead, you can use these steps to copy a selected object to a new layer, leaving the Background layer unchanged.

3 Click

Start

1 Click

2 Click

1 With an image open in the Editor's Full Edit mode, click a selection tool, such as Lasso.

2 Carefully select the object to be copied to a new layer.

3 Choose **Layer**, **New**, **Layer via Copy** or press **Ctrl+J**.

End

 TIP
Cutting a Selection
The command Layer, New, Layer via Cut works just the same way, but it also deletes the selection from the original layer. Especially if the original layer is the Background, use Layer via Copy instead.

 TIP
Deleting or Hiding
As long as the original layer is intact, you can always hide or delete the copied layer (choose **Layer**, **Delete Layer** or drag the layer's entry in the Layers palette to the Trash button) to cancel all its changes with a click.

REPOSITIONING A LAYER

When you moved text and shapes in previous tasks, you might not have realized you were actually repositioning an entire layer, including not only the selection but also the transparent pixels surrounding it. In this image, the cat and the menu board are on separate layers, and the task moves the cat's layer lower in the image.

Start

2 Click

3 Click and drag

1 Click

1 In the Editor's Full Edit mode, click the name of the layer in the Layers palette.

2 Switch to the **Move** tool.

3 Click and drag the layer to reposition it in relation to the image area (or nudge it with the arrow keys, or **Shift-click** to constrain it to 45-degree angles as you drag).

End

NOTE
Auto Select Layer
If Auto Select Layer is checked in the Move tool's options bar, the layer selection (the active layer) changes automatically when you click an object that resides on it. Remember that doing so actually moves the entire layer, not just the object.

TIP
More Button
Clicking the little triangular More button in the upper-right corner of the Layers palette brings up a menu of commands that affect layers (a handy alternative to the Layers menu).

CONTROLLING LAYERS

The icons and buttons in the Layers palette control various layer behaviors such as locking a layer (preventing changes), creating and deleting a layer, hiding/unhiding a layer, new fill/adjustment layers, and linking layers.

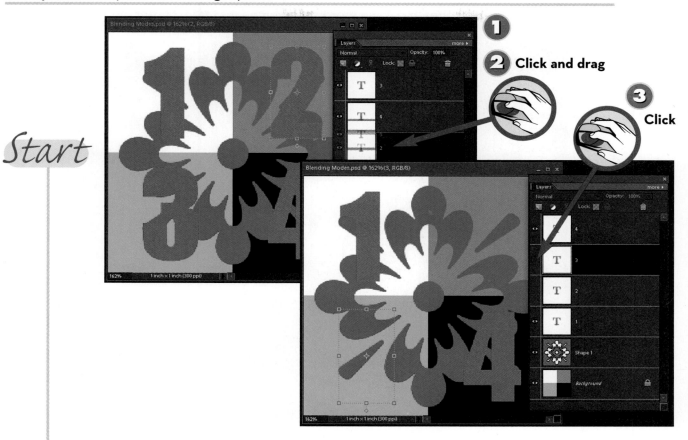

2 Click and drag

3 Click

Start

End

1 In the Editor's Full Edit mode, open or undock the Layers palette (or choose **Window**, **Layers**).

2 To change the order of layers, click and drag the layer name to a new position, higher or lower on the list.

3 To hide any layer, causing it not to display or print, click the **Eye** icon. (To restore its visibility, click the **Eye** icon again.)

CREATING A FILL LAYER AND ADJUSTING LAYER OPACITY

One way to change how layers look is to adjust the *opacity* of a fill layer above them. Think of a *semitransparent* fill layer (less than 100% opacity) as a colored photographic filter—tinting and dimming the layers beneath it. (The more opaque, the less transparent, and vice versa.)

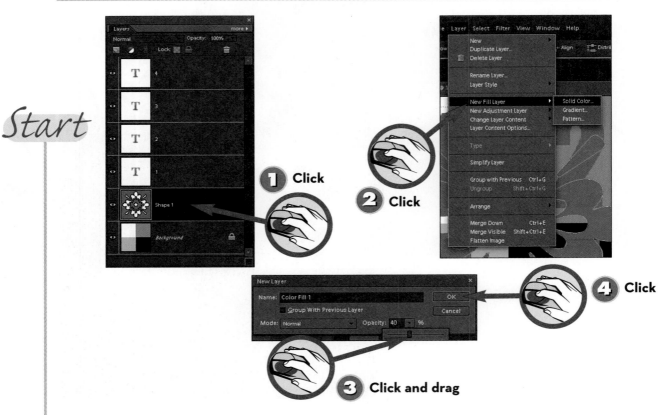

1 Click

2 Click

3 Click and drag

4 Click

1 In the Editor's Full Edit mode, click the layer in the Layers palette above which the new layer will be inserted.

2 Choose **Layer**, **New Fill Layer**, **Solid Color**.

3 Click and drag the **Opacity** slider to change how transparent the new layer is.

4 Click **OK**.

Continued

-NOTE-
To Bin or Not to Bin
Drag a palette out of the Palette Bin if you want to move it around on the screen. That way you can put it right next to the area of the image you're working on, or you can close the Palette Bin to enlarge your work area.

-NOTE-
Well Adjusted
Continuing to add other adjustment and fill layers, each with its own properties, will have a combined effect. Remember that an adjustment layer affects only the appearance of the layers *beneath* it.

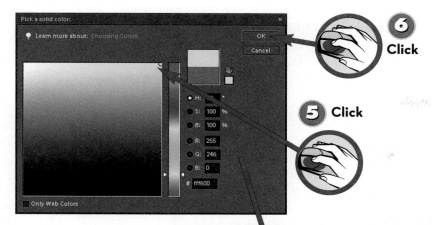

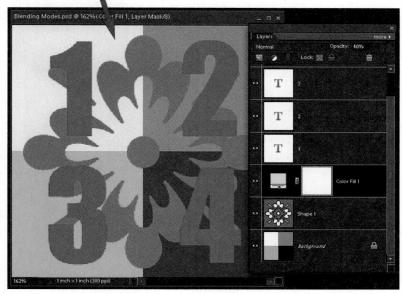

5 Click

6 Click

5 Click to choose a fill color.

6 Click **OK**.

End

NOTE

Gradient and Pattern Fills

Besides Solid Color, other submenu selections available in step 2 are Gradient and Pattern, which have the same options as the Gradient tool and the Pattern settings of the Paint Bucket tool.

TIP

Special Effects

By using either the Gradient or Pattern submenu commands rather than Solid Color, you can create variegated effects: Gradient could cause the filtration effect to fade across the background; Pattern could give it a texture (a dust storm, for instance).

FLIPPING OR ROTATING A LAYER

The purpose of flipping or rotating a layer can be either to change the position of the objects on the layer or to vary the effect of a gradient or pattern layer. The Image, Rotate command has a submenu section for such operations performed on entire layers.

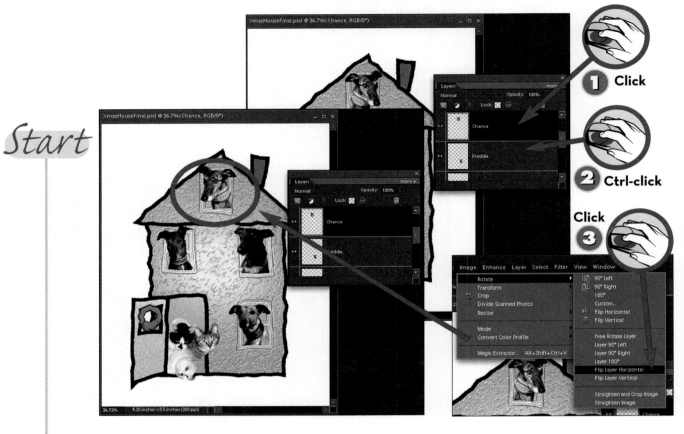

1. In the Editor's Full Edit mode, click the layer name in the Layers palette to make it the *active*, or current, layer.

2. Optionally, **Ctrl-click** layer names in the Layers palette to select any other layers that must be included in the operation.

3. Choose **Image**, **Rotate** and choose from the second group of submenu commands, such as Flip Layer Horizontal.

TIP
Selections or Layers?
When part of the image within a layer—such as a shape or text—is selected, the second group of commands in the Image, Rotate submenu switches from Layer to Selection. They have the same effect, but only on the selected area.

ADDING AN ADJUSTMENT LAYER

An adjustment layer has no color of its own, but it does let you control color, brightness/contrast, and other factors on layers beneath without making changes directly to them. The adjustment layer has no effect on layers above it.

Start

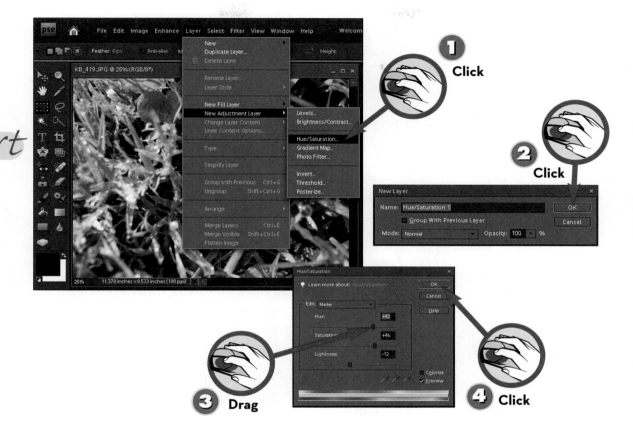

① Click

② Click

③ Drag

④ Click

① In the Editor's Full Edit mode, with a layer active, choose **Layer**, **New Adjustment Layer** and choose from the submenu commands, such as Hue/Saturation.

② Click **OK**.

③ Make adjustments using the options in the dialog box and see the effect on your image in the background.

④ When you are satisfied with the effect, click **OK**.

End

TIP
Select a Layer First
The new adjustment layer will be inserted just above the layer that's active when you begin step 1. So, if you want to adjust the background image, select that layer first and then complete these steps.

NOTE
Blending Mode
As described in the next task, the effect of any fill or adjustment layer can also be controlled by choosing a blending mode from the Mode menu in the Layers palette (or Mode menu in the New Layer dialog box).

CHANGING LAYER BLENDING MODES

A blending mode controls how pixel values within a layer are blended with those of the layers beneath. The default is Normal. Other modes include Dissolve, several Dodge or Burn effects, quality of light (such as Soft or Hard), and adding (Exclusion) or subtracting (Difference) pixel values or individual elements of color.

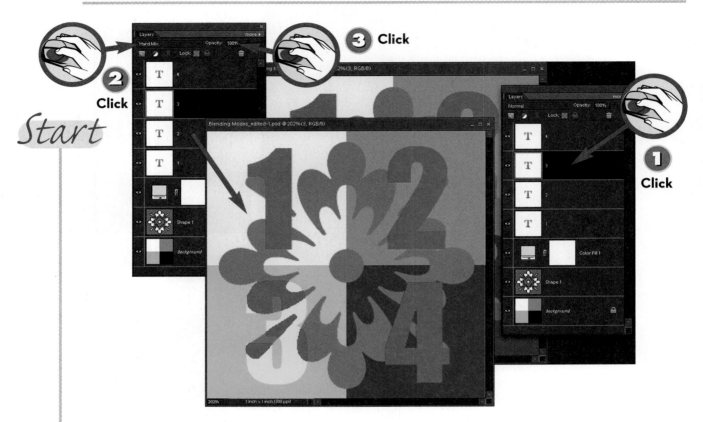

Start

End

1. In the Editor's Full Edit mode, click a layer name in the Layers palette to make it the active layer.

2. Choose a blending mode, such as Hard Mix.

3. Adjust the **Opacity** setting to control the extent of blending.

TIP
Try 'Em On
After making a choice from the blending mode list in step 2, press the **up-** or **down-arrow** key to step through the other modes and preview their effects on the image.

TIP
Controlling Blending Modes
To turn off a blending mode, change the setting back to **Normal** for that layer in the pop-up menu in the upper-left corner of the Layers palette. To make a layer fully opaque again, just restore its Opacity setting to 100% in the upper-right corner of that palette.

COPYING AND PASTING A LAYER STYLE

Copying layer styles is particularly convenient when you've made several style changes on one layer and want to apply them with a click to all objects on another layer—also if you've taken pains to fine-tune a style, such as having adjusted the angle of a drop shadow.

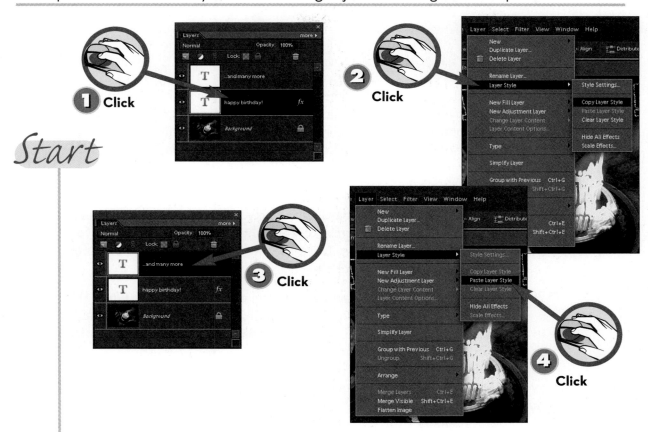

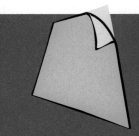

1. In the Editor's Full Edit mode, choose a layer that contains a layer style (such as Drop Shadow) from the Layers palette.

2. Choose **Layer, Layer Style, Copy Layer Style**.

3. Click the name of a layer to which the style will be applied.

4. Choose **Layer, Layer Style, Paste Layer Style**.

End

TIP

Fine-Tuning Styles

To fine-tune a layer style on the active layer, such as Bevel or Drop Shadow, choose **Layer, Layer Style, Style Settings**. Make adjustments by clicking and dragging the sliders, and then click **OK**.

CREATING SNAZZY EFFECTS

With the invention of the electronic calculator, schoolchildren are the only ones who fret over doing arithmetic by hand. Similarly, you might be surprised at how many commercial artists don't draw from scratch anymore. Many of them earn their daily bread using computer graphics software such as Photoshop Elements to make photos look like fine art.

When you've worked through the tasks in this Part, you'll know many of their secrets. You can make greeting cards and party invitations look as if they were hand-drawn by a skilled sketch artist, create photorealistic illustrations for flyers and newsletters, and add expensive-looking graphics that give a professional touch to your personal Website.

Photoshop Elements helps you achieve artistic effects by way of *filters* that can transform an image with a click, but in complex ways. The program comes with a wide variety of filters, and you can download even more of them (called plug-ins) from www.adobe.com and other vendors' Websites. There are far too many filters to cover them all here, but you'll see enough to show you how easy they are to apply—and to start you thinking about all the creative possibilities.

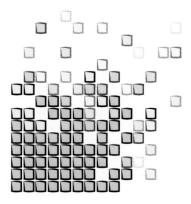

HOW DID YOU DO *THAT*?

Before It helps to start with a photo that has an interesting composition, and some bright colors and contrasts.

After Here's some "fine art" that took less than a minute to make. It's the result of adding both the Palette Knife artistic filter and a Sandstone texture, and finally adjusting Hue for brighter greenery.

ADDING A DECORATIVE BORDER

A frame is just one example of the wide variety of custom, prebuilt shapes available in Photoshop Elements. To make the frame even fancier, this example applies a Craquelure filter to give the frame a rich, dimensional look.

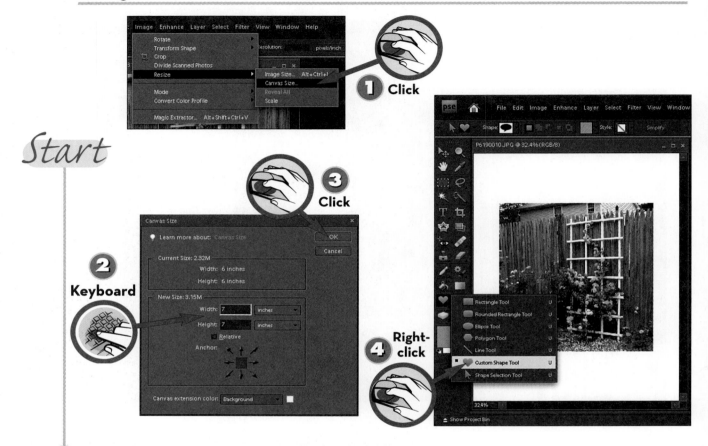

Start

1. With the Editor in Full Edit mode and an image open, choose **Image**, **Resize**, **Canvas Size**.

2. Type a Width the same as the print size and about 2 inches wider than the current image size. Do the same for Height.

3. Click **OK**.

4. Right-click the **Shape** tool in the toolbar and choose **Custom Shape Tool**.

Continued

NOTE

Know the Image Size

In this example, the image size of the photo is about 5 × 7 inches. Placing it on an 8 × 10 canvas adds just the right amount of border for the decorative frame.

Click **5**

Double-click **6**

Click **8**

Click and drag **7**

5 In the options bar, open the Shape pop-up palette.

6 Double-click any Frame shape.

7 With the Foreground color set to the color you want the frame to be, click and drag in the image to surround the photo with the frame.

8 Click the **Simplify** button.

Continued

 TIP

Want More Custom Shapes?
To pick from a variety of frame shapes, when the Shape pop-up palette is open in steps 5 and 6, click the circular arrow button and choose **All Elements Shapes** from the pop-up menu.

The frame used here is just one of many Custom Shapes, which are ready-made so that you don't have to do any freehand drawing. Categories include Animals, Arrows, Banners and Awards, Characters, Default, Frames, Fruit, Music, Nature, Objects, Ornaments, Shapes, Signs, Symbols, Talk Bubbles, and Tiles.

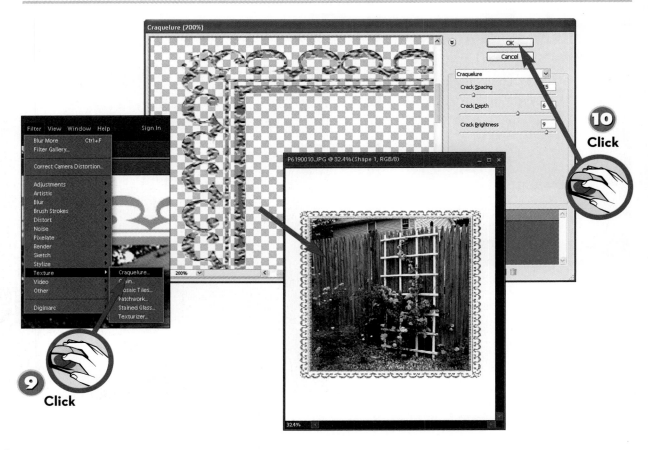

Click

10
Click

9 Choose **Filter, Texture, Craquelure**.

10 Click **OK** again.

End

TIP
Craquelure Not Your Style?
Instead of applying the Craquelure filter in step 9, try any other effect or combination of effects from the Filter menu.

TIP
Don't See the Preview?
For the preview of the whole frame to be visible in the Craquelure dialog box in step 10, click the – button several times to reduce the view percentage from 100% to 14%.

CREATING A GRADIENT FILL

A *gradient fill* is a blended transition—usually between two colors—within a selected area. In this example, the gradient is applied to the entire background, but it could also be used to fill any object you select, even hollow text.

1 Click

Start

2 Click

3 Click

4 Click and drag

1 With the Editor in Full Edit mode and an image open, choose the **Quick Selection** tool, or press **A**.

2 Click to select the area in the image to which the effect will be applied.

3 Choose the **Gradient** tool, or press **G**.

4 Click and drag across the area to be filled in the direction you want the color gradation to take. (Press **Ctrl+D** to release the selection.)

End

TIP

Making Your Selection

Use any combination of selection tools in step 1 (Magic Wand, Lassos, or Marquees). Press **Shift** as you select with a tool to add an area to the current selection, **Alt** to subtract.

TIP

Mix Your Own Gradients

After switching to the Gradient tool, clicking the **Edit** button in the options bar opens the Gradient Editor, which contains options for creating custom gradients.

ADDING A VIGNETTE TO A PORTRAIT

Somehow, putting a soft edge around the subject of a portrait just seems to make the image more special. It's a traditional darkroom technique that's incredibly easy to emulate with Photoshop Elements.

Start

1 Right-click

2 Click

3 Click and drag

4 Click

1 With a picture open, right-click the **Rectangular Marquee** tool.

2 Choose the **Elliptical Marquee** tool.

3 Click and drag in the image to draw an oval selection marquee.

4 Choose **Select**, **Inverse** or press **Shift+Ctrl+I**.

Continued

 TIP
Keep Trying
The amount of feathering you add depends on the resolution and size of the image; you might have to try a few different settings before you're satisfied. Don't forget that you can use the Undo History palette to back up and try again.

 NOTE
Getting in Shape
Don't feel that you have to stick to creating an oval vignette—that's just the most traditional shape. Experiment with other shapes, including using the Lasso tool to draw a freeform selection.

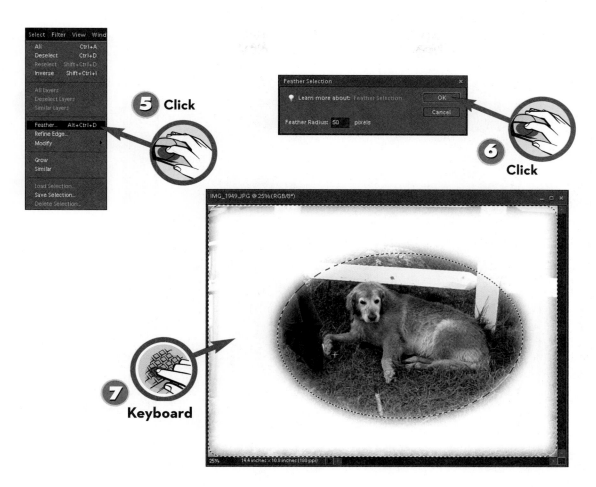

5 Choose **Select**, **Feather** or press **Alt+Ctrl+D**.

6 Enter a number of pixels in the Feather Radius field and click **OK**.

7 Press **Delete** to remove the background.

End

NOTE

Going Way, Way Back

For a really old-fashioned feel, combine this vignette effect with a sepia tone effect. Check out the tip on **p. 204** for instructions.

TIP

Tidying Up

To center the vignetted photo in the image, invert the selection after step 7 and choose **Image**, **Crop**. That gets rid of the photo's asymmetrical white border.

CREATING A HIGH-CONTRAST BLACK-AND-WHITE PICTURE

Back in the ancient days of film, high-contrast (hi-con) transparencies were called *Kodaliths*, the name of a Kodak product for mastering printing plates. You can create some dramatic artistic effects doing the same thing digitally—by converting a photo to black-and-white, with no shading.

(1) With the Editor in Full Edit mode and an image open, choose **Image, Mode, Grayscale**.

(2) Click **OK** on the warning dialog box.

(3) Choose **Enhance, Adjust Lighting, Brightness/Contrast**.

Continued

NOTE

Don't Do This to Your Dad

Hi-con doesn't make flattering portraits. Clean-shaven men with five o'clock shadow end up with real stubble trouble, and wispy laugh lines become deep trenches.

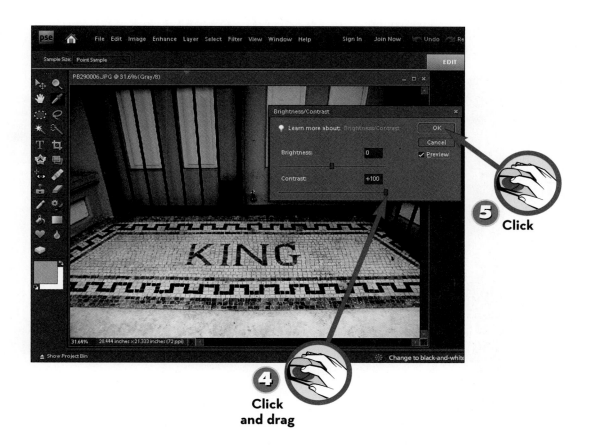

⑤ Click

④
**Click
and drag**

④ Adjust the **Contrast** slider to **100**.

⑤ Click **OK**.

End

TIP

Adjust Brightness

In step 4, after increasing Contrast, it might also be necessary to adjust the Brightness slider a bit, as done here.

NOTE

Consider the Source

Hi-con effects work best on images with smooth surfaces and sharp edges, such as architectural views. If the source photo has shaded areas, keep the Contrast setting below 80% to preserve some grayscale.

FADING OUT COLOR

You'll often see this effect used in advertising—it's a neat way to convey the idea of an object moving from the past to the present, or from a humdrum world into an exciting one. One side of the image is black and white, and the other side is full color, with a smooth transition between the two modes in the middle.

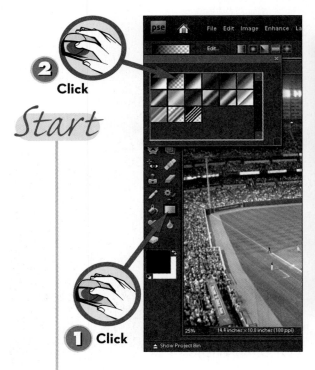

2 Click

Start

1 Click

3 Click

4 Click and drag

1 Click to choose the **Gradient** tool, or press **G**.

2 Making sure that the foreground color is black, choose the **Foreground to Transparent** gradient in the options bar.

3 Choose **Saturation** from the Mode pop-up menu on the options bar.

4 Click and drag horizontally across the middle of the photo.

End

NOTE

Messing Around

Try different Mode settings and different gradients to see what other interesting results you can come up with. You can also set the Gradient tool to generate one of the four other gradient shapes, such as radial.

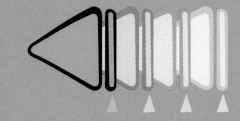

COLORING A SINGLE OBJECT

Remember the striking image of the little girl's pink coat in the black and white movie *Schindler's List*? One color object really stands out against a black-and-white background. Here's how to achieve that effect in your own photos.

Start

Click (1)

Click (2)

Click (3)

Click (4)

① Click to choose the **Selection Brush**.

② With the **Selection Brush**, paint over the object you want to leave in color.

③ After the selection is made, choose **Select**, **Inverse**.

④ Choose **Enhance**, **Adjust Color**, **Remove Color** or press **Shift+Ctrl+U**.

End

TIP

Bonus Points

For an extra color boost, choose **Enhance, Adjust Color, Adjust Hue/Saturation** after step 2. Drag the **Saturation** slider to the right to make the one colored object even more vivid.

NOTE

It's All About You

You can use any tool to create the selection in step 1; the Magic Selection Brush, the Lasso, and the Magic Wand are all good choices. Use whichever tool you're most comfortable with.

DELETING THE BACKGROUND

Backgrounds can be useful, but they can also be distracting. When you want to pull an object out of its environment by removing its background, turn to the Magic Extractor.

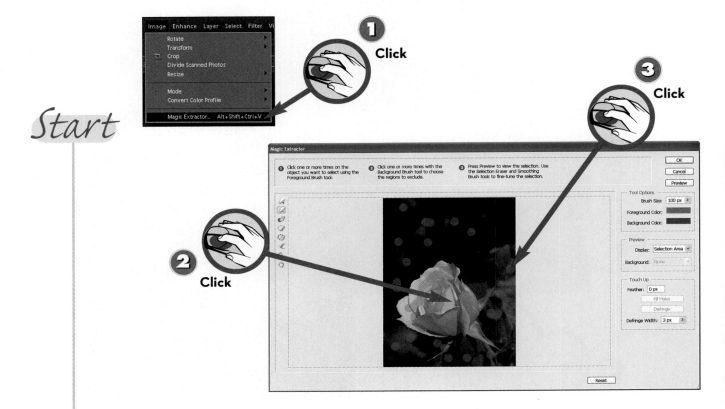

 Start

1 With the photo open, choose **Image**, **Magic Extractor** or press **Alt+Shift+Ctrl+V**.

2 With the **Foreground Brush** tool, click several times or scribble on the object you want to keep.

3 With the **Background Brush** tool, click several times or scribble on the rest of the image.

 Continued

NOTE
Almost the Same
This technique works similarly to the Quick Selection tool. The dialog box's instructions say to click the areas you want to indicate as background and foreground, but scribbling works just as well.

TIP
Best Bets
You'll achieve the best results when you use an image that has a distinct foreground object that's very different in color or in lightness from the background.

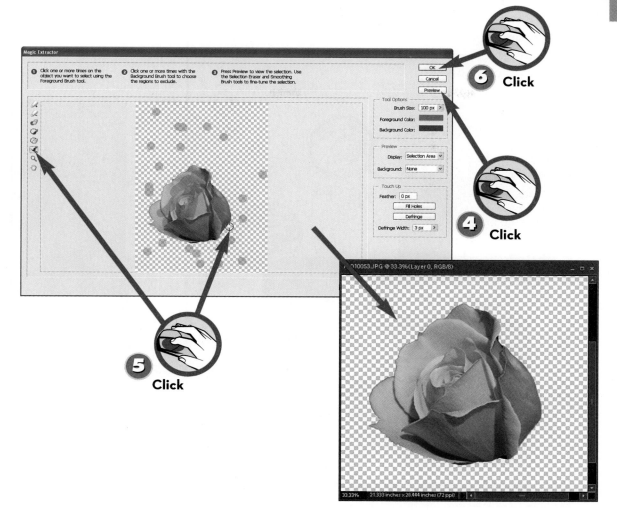

4 Click **Preview** to see how the object looks with the background removed.

5 Use the **Selection Eraser** and the **Smoothing Brush** tools to delete leftover background areas or restore missing foreground areas.

6 Click **OK** to finalize the background removal.

End

NOTE
Go Back, Go Back

Take as long as you need to complete step 5; this is where the quick-and-dirty jobs are separated from the truly professional-looking ones.

TIP
Background Notes

After you remove the photo's background, you can choose **Layer, Flatten Image** to replace the transparent pixels with the background color. Or, if you prefer, you can drag the image into another photo to give it a new background.

MAKING A PHOTO LOOK LIKE AN OIL PAINTING

No one's proposing you start cranking out fake Rembrandts, but there's something about brushstrokes on canvas that says high class. Try this with the family portrait and pretend you sat for a Dutch master.

Start

1. With the Editor in Full Edit mode and an image open, choose **Filter**, **Brush Strokes**, **Angled Strokes**.

2. Adjust the **Direction Balance**, **Stroke Length**, and **Sharpness** sliders until you achieve a combination of settings you like.

3. When you see the desired effect in the Preview window, click **OK**.

4. Choose **Filter**, **Texture**, **Texturizer**.

Continued

 TIP

Tuning Your Strokes

The slider options in step 2 control the magnitude of the effect. You want to balance making the brushstrokes obvious enough to be seen, yet not so much as to obliterate fine detail in the picture.

5 From the Texture pop-up menu, choose **Canvas**.

6 Click **OK**.

End

TIP

How Rough Is Your Canvas?

As with brushstrokes, you can adjust Texturizer options to control roughness and lighting on the canvas: Scaling, Relief, and Light Direction. The Invert option reverses light and dark effects.

NOTE

No Rules

There are no rules for applying artistic effects. Be guided by your own taste. For example, instead of a Canvas texture, try Burlap or Sandstone. And remember, results vary depending on the source material.

POSTERIZING A PICTURE

Posterization became popular in the psychedelic movement of the 1960s as a way of making images seem more intense. Photoshop Elements includes a filter called Poster Edges to create this effect.

Start

2 Click and drag

3 Click

1 Click

End

1 With the Editor in Full Edit mode and an image open, choose **Filter**, **Artistic**, **Poster Edges**.

2 Adjust the sliders for **Edge Thickness**, **Edge Intensity**, and **Posterization** until you like the look of the image.

3 Click **OK**.

TIP

Ideas for Greeting Cards?

Applying the Poster Edges effect to a photo can make it look like a fine watercolor and ink drawing, or an elaborate illustration in a children's book.

MAKING A PHOTO LOOK LIKE A SKETCH

Whether your drawings look like stick figures or you're just in too big a hurry to sit down with your sketchpad, Photoshop Elements can make any photo look hand-drawn. For example, take a photo of the curbside view of your home, convert it to a sketch, and use it to illustrate personalized party invitations or stationery.

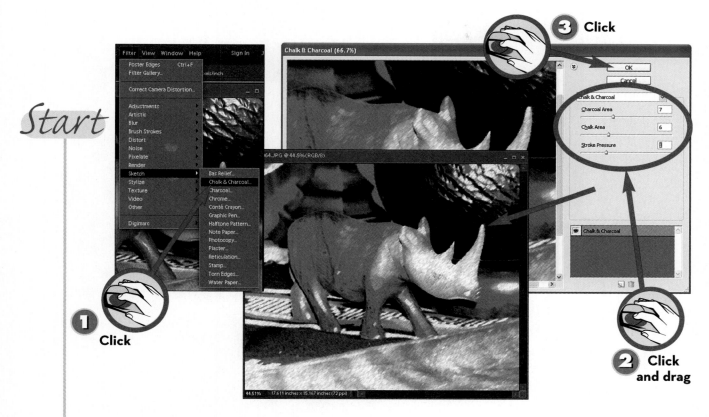

Start

1 **Click**

2 **Click and drag**

3 **Click**

End

1 With the Editor in Full Edit mode and an image open, choose **Filter**, **Sketch**, **Chalk & Charcoal**.

2 Adjust the sliders for **Charcoal Area**, **Chalk Area**, and **Stroke Pressure** until the image looks right to you.

3 Click **OK**.

TIP

Make It Snappy

Although level correction isn't a required step, it's applied to this example to darken the lines so that the result reproduces better in print.

APPLYING THE POINTILLIZE FILTER

Pointillism is a technique pioneered by French Impressionist painter Georges Seurat more than a century ago. His paintings are composed of thousands of tiny dots of bright colors—and the overall effect is apparent only when viewing the work from a distance. In a sense, he invented pixels, which are the building blocks of today's computerized, digital images.

Start

Click ①

②
**Click
and drag**

③ **Click**

① With the Editor in Full Edit mode and an image open, choose **Filter**, **Pixelate**, **Pointillize**.

② Adjust the **Cell Size** slider to get the look you want.

③ Click **OK**.

End

TIP

How Big Is a Cell?

Cell size in step 2 controls the size of the picture dots and the magnitude of the effect. You want it large enough to make the effect visible, small enough to preserve important picture details.

TRIMMING A PHOTO INTO A CUSTOM SHAPE

Who says photographs have to be square or rectangular? The sky's the limit as far as the Photoshop Elements Cookie Cutter tool is concerned, so you can make the shape of the photo part of the message it communicates. Try them all!

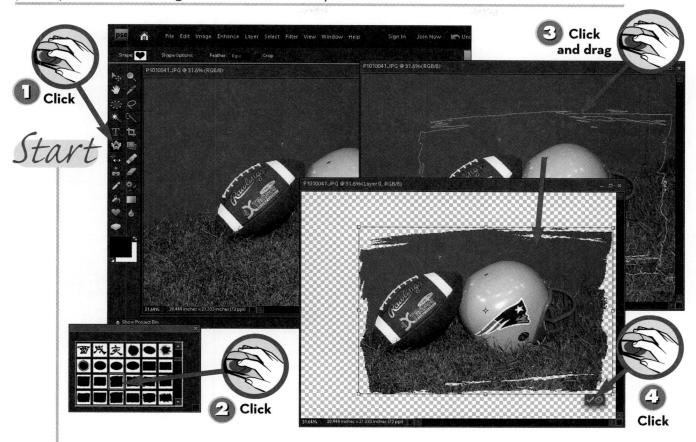

Start

End

1. With an image open in the Editor's Full Edit mode, choose the **Cookie Cutter** tool from the toolbox.

2. Click to open the **Shape** pop-up menu, and then select a shape.

3. Click and drag in the document window to create the shape.

4. Click the **Commit** button to hide the parts of the image outside the shape.

TIP

Cutting and Cropping

After you've applied the Cookie Cutter tool to your image, you might want to use the Crop tool to get rid of the extra empty space surrounding the new shape.

NOTE

There's Time to Get It Right

Until you press Enter, click the Commit button on the options bar, or switch to another tool or layer, you can move and resize the shape as much as you want to perfectly frame your picture.

APPLYING EFFECTS WITH THE SMART BRUSH

Using the Photoshop Elements new Smart Brush, you can apply special effects with a paint-brush, putting them right where you want them and nowhere else. It's a great tool for cleaning up snapshots with a minimum of fuss.

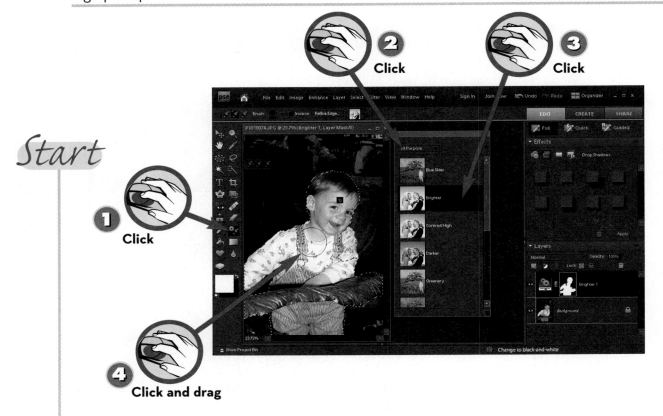

Click ②

Click ③

Start

Click ①

Click and drag ④

① With an image open in the Editor's Full Edit mode, click the **Smart Brush** tool.

② Choose an effects category from the pop-up menu at the top of the Smart Paint palette.

③ Click an effect to apply.

④ Paint over the area to which you want to apply the effect.

Continued

NOTE
Layers on Layers
The Smart Brush adds adjustment layers to your image, combined with layer masks that determine where the adjustments are visible and where they're hidden. To learn more about adjustment layers, flip back to "Adding an Adjustment Layer" in Part 6.

NOTE
Do It Now or Do It Later
You can return to a Smart Brush adjustment at any time to modify its settings. When you click the corresponding layer in the Layers palette, Photoshop Elements restores the Smart Brush selection.

5 Click

6 Click and drag

Double-click **7**

8 Click

5 To remove an area from the selection, click the **Remove from Selection** brush.

6 Paint over the area that shouldn't have the effect.

7 To modify the settings, double-click the **Pin** in the image window or the layer's thumbnail in the Layers palette.

8 Make your changes and click **OK**.

End

NOTE

It Takes All Kinds

The effects you can apply with the Smart Brush fall into several categories; some are "fixes" for common image problems, and others are special effects to jazz up your images. Be sure to explore all your options.

TOUCHING UP WITH THE DETAIL SMART BRUSH

The Detail Smart Brush works the same way as the Smart Brush, only instead of helping you make your selection the way the Quick Selection tool does, it only goes where you put it, so you have more control. This tool is great for fixing up small areas where you need to make sure that the effect is applied exactly where you want it and nowhere else.

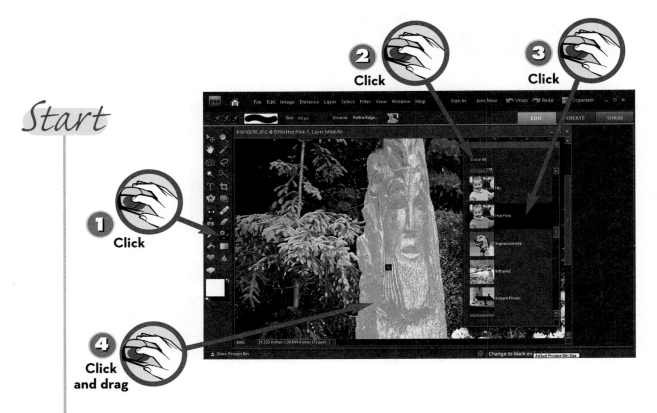

Start

② Click

③ Click

① Click

④ Click and drag

① With an image open in the Editor's Full Edit mode, click the **Detail Smart Brush** tool.

② Choose an effects category from the pop-up menu at the top of the Smart Paint palette.

③ Click an effect to apply.

④ Paint over the area to which you want to apply the effect.

Continued

NOTE
Just Like Big Sister
The Detail Smart Brush can apply all the same effects as the Smart Brush; be sure to explore all the options in the Smart Paint palette.

TIP
A Little of Both
The Detail Smart Brush works like a Painting tool; it has settings for brush size and shape in the options bar. But it also works like a Selection tool; you can click Refine Edge in the options bar to modify the selection's shape and size.

5 Click

6 Click and drag

7 Double-click

8 Click

5 To remove an area from the selection, click the **Remove from Selection** brush.

6 Paint over the area that shouldn't have the effect.

7 To modify the settings, double-click the **Pin** in the image window.

8 Make your changes and click **OK**.

End

NOTE

Getting Back

To make changes to an existing Smart Paint effect, **Ctrl-click** or right-click its **Pin** to reactivate the selection. If a Pin is located inconveniently, you can click and drag to move it.

TIP

Same Tune, New Words

If you want to add more than one effect with either of the Smart Brushes, choose **Reset Tool** from the pop-up menu at the left end of the options bar, and then choose a new effect.

PAINTING AND DRAWING

Many people think of Photoshop Elements mainly as a digital photo lab, but it's also an art studio. So, welcome to your all-electronic work-and-play room—where you never have to wear a smock or clean a brush.

Those of you who start with a photo as a background may have a more practical purpose in mind—such as making ads and brochures. And along with adding text, combining your photos with your original artwork gives a wonderfully personal touch. Recipients of your greeting cards, party invitations, photo email, and newsletters will appreciate the care you took—even though none of this is nearly as hard as they might imagine!

Getting a bit more serious, you can also illustrate business presentations, school reports, and instructional materials with professional-looking diagrams and drawings. No more crude pencil sketches, and good-bye forever to stick figures!

But don't stop there. Set aside a rainy weekend afternoon to discover the joy of digital painting and drawing. Vincent Van Gogh never had such a rich and varied set of tools!

LOOK WHAT I MADE!

8th Annual
GREYHOUND
FESTIVAL
GREYHOUND PLACEMENT SERVICE
OF NEW HAMPSHIRE

VOTE GREYHOUND IN 2004!

This event logo was drawn and colored entirely in Photoshop Elements. Who needs paper and paints when you have pixels?

CREATING A SHAPE

Photoshop Elements generates a variety of geometric shapes for you. Here we show drawing over an image. You can also start by choosing **File**, **New**, **Blank Image** to draw on a blank canvas.

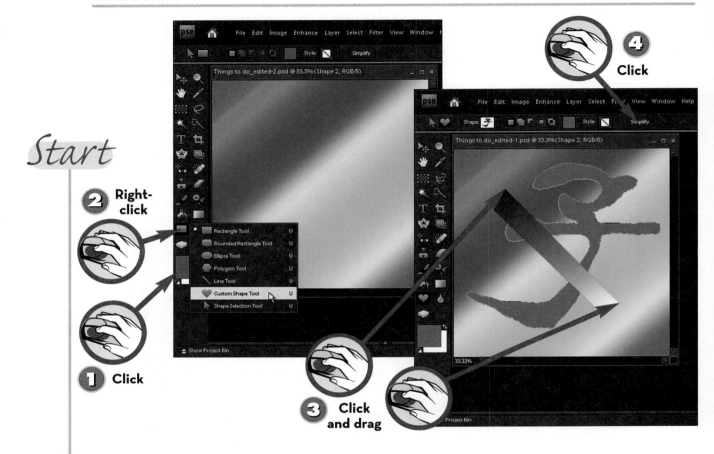

Start

End

1. With an image open in the Editor's Full Edit mode, click to choose a foreground color.

2. Right-click the **Shape** tool and choose the shape tool you want, such as the Custom Shape tool. If you're using the Custom Shape tool, choose the specific shape you want in the Options bar.

3. Click and drag in the image area to adjust the size and proportions of the shape.

4. To make the pixels of the shape editable, click the **Simplify** button.

TIP

Shift to Get Regular

Hold down the **Shift** key after you've started drawing to make Rectangles square, Ellipses circular. Lines follow the closest 45° angle.

NOTE

Moving and Resizing

To move or resize a shape before it's simplified, use the Shape Selection tool. When simplified, use the Move tool instead. For best-quality shapes, always try to resize before you simplify, rather than after.

ADDING A BEVEL TO A SHAPE

New shapes can look plain and flat. Adding a bevel gives the shape a dimensional quality that can also make it stand out from the background. Photoshop Elements provides a nice selection of bevel styles that can give your object a bold, dimensional look. Just click the one you like, and it's applied automatically.

Click

Start

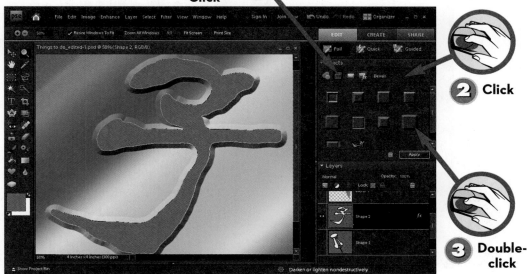

2 Click

3 Double-click

1. With a shape selected, click the **Layer Styles** button at the top of the Effects palette.

2. Choose **Bevels** in the Style Libraries pop-up menu.

3. Double-click the bevel style you want to apply.

End

TIP

Free Samples
If you don't like the bevel style you apply, just click another thumbnail to apply a different style—you don't have to remove the first bevel before changing it.

TIP

Selecting Shapes
If the shape you want isn't the most recent one you created, select it with the **Move** tool before you do step 1. (**Auto Select Layer** must be checked.) If the shape is one of many on a layer, use the **Shape Selection** tool instead.

FILLING A SHAPE WITH COLOR

If you've worked through the tasks to this point, this won't be the first time you've used the Paint Bucket tool. But notice how quickly and easily you can recolor a shape. Always remember that the Paint Bucket—like other painting tools—uses whatever you've set as the current foreground color.

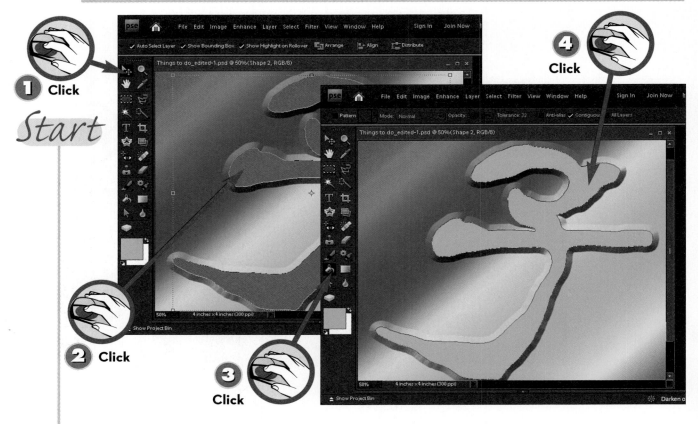

1 Click

Start

2 Click

3 Click

4 Click

1 Having chosen the foreground color, switch to the **Move** tool, or press **V**. (**Auto Select Layer** must be checked.)

2 Click to select the shape.

3 Switch to the **Paint Bucket** tool, or press **K**.

4 Click inside the shape to apply the color.

End

TIP
Change the Fill Color
Before you do step 1, click the **Foreground** color swatch at the bottom of the toolbar and make a selection from the Color Picker.

TIP
Fill with a Pattern
If you prefer a pattern rather than a color, before doing step 4 choose **Pattern** from the Fill pop-up menu in the options bar; then make a selection from the Pattern menu.

CHOOSING A COLOR FROM THE IMAGE

Want to pick a color for a new shape or brush stroke that exactly matches some color in the image? The Eyedropper tool sucks up the color you click and loads it as the current foreground color. Whatever painting or drawing tool you use next applies that color.

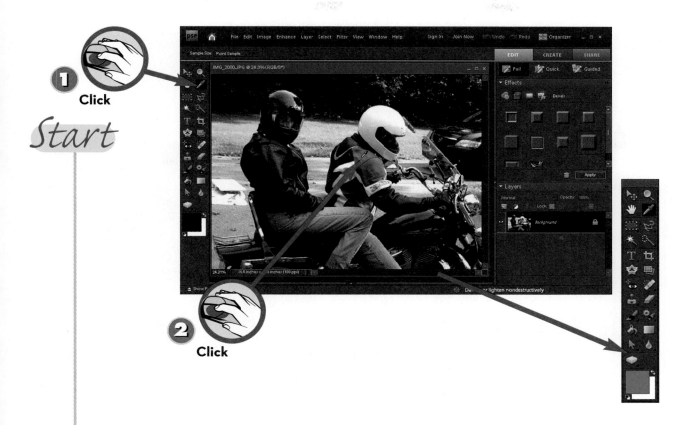

Start

1 Click

2 Click

End

1 Click the **Eyedropper** tool, or press **I**.

2 Click a color you want to match in the image area. The Foreground color changes to the color of your sample, and you can now use it with any tool that applies color.

TIP
Changing Sample Size
Before step 2, you can choose 3 by 3 Average or 5 by 5 Average on the Options bar to set the number of pixels in the area the Eyedropper will sample. (It's an average, so the resulting color may be a blend of the sampled pixels.)

NOTE
Whenever You See It
Photoshop Elements uses the Eyedropper pointer in other places, such as the Color Swatches palette, and it always works as a color selector.

USING THE COLOR SWATCHES PALETTE

If you've ever browsed through color swatches at the paint store, you know how handy it can be to see a coordinated set of choices. It's generally quicker and easier to make a choice from preset color swatches than to use the Color Picker (which, for most folks, has way too many).

Start

Click ❶

Click ❷

End

❶ Choose **Window**, **Color Swatches**.

❷ Click the color you want to use next. The foreground color changes to the color of your sample, and you are ready to use any tool that applies color.

 TIP

Rolling Your Own

You can save your own favorite colors in the Swatches palette. To save the current foreground color, scroll down to the blank area at the bottom of the palette and click to add a swatch.

PAINTING AND DRAWING WITH A BRUSH AND PENCIL

Use the Brush tool to do freehand painting (or Impressionist Brush to paint over and blur an existing image). The Pencil tool right beside it in the toolbar works much the same, except pencil lines don't have soft edges.

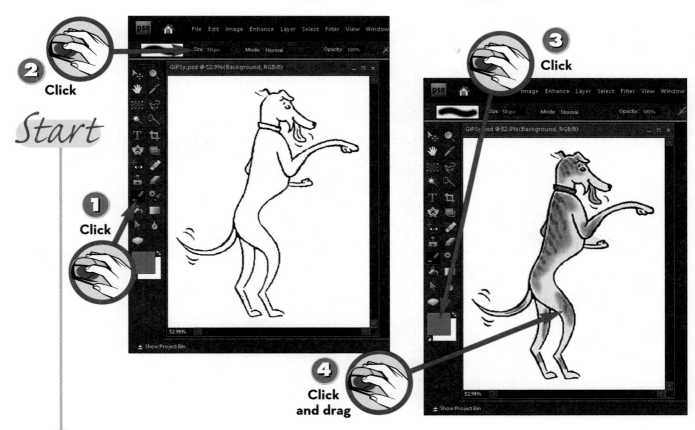

Start

End

1. Choose the **Brush** tool.

2. Set brush properties in the options bar, such as Size.

3. Choose a foreground color.

4. Click and drag in the image area to apply each brush stroke.

NOTE
Brush Stroke Technique

Keep holding down the mouse button and paint with a scrubbing motion to apply a single, continuous brush stroke. Or, click and release the mouse button frequently as you paint to apply dabs of color.

TIP
A Tip on Brush Tips

Choose the tip size and brush stroke properties in the options bar before you do step 2. Pick one of the preset brushes or adjust the other options to create your own.

CONTROLLING HOW BRUSHES BEHAVE

If you really want to get arty with brush tips, you can make all kinds of adjustments in the options bar, before you start painting. Also located there is the Airbrush button, which generates a spray of pixels at the brush tip. (Access the full range of options from the More Options pop-up menu.)

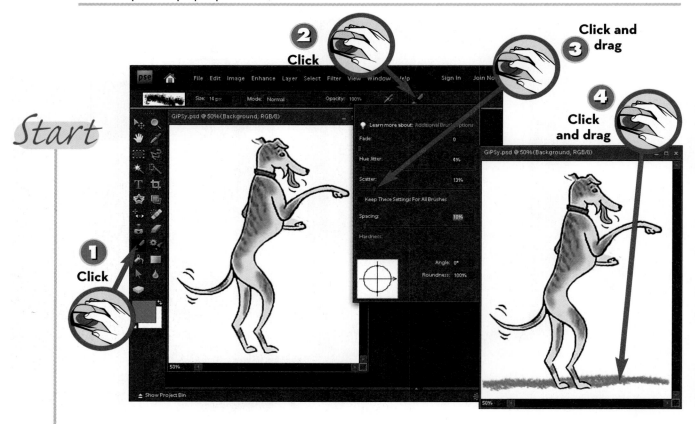

Start

End

① Switch to the **Brush** tool.

② Click **More Options** in the options bar.

③ Adjust how the brush works by dragging a slider or typing a new percentage for one or more options.

④ Click and drag in the image area to apply each brush stroke.

 TIP
Lots to Choose From
The options bar contains more than a dozen categories of preset brushes, and you have the choice of fine-tuning any of them by making adjustments using the More Options pop-up menu.

 TIP
Still More Options
In the options bar, Mode controls effects for artistic purposes, as well as for doing fine photo retouching. Opacity, in effect, is paint thickness—lower numbers are more like watercolor.

PAINTING WITH THE PATTERN STAMP

Painting with a pattern is lots of fun—and something you can't do nearly as easily with physical paint and paper. The result is more like making cutouts of wallpaper or fabric and pasting them down—much like collage and mixed-media art techniques.

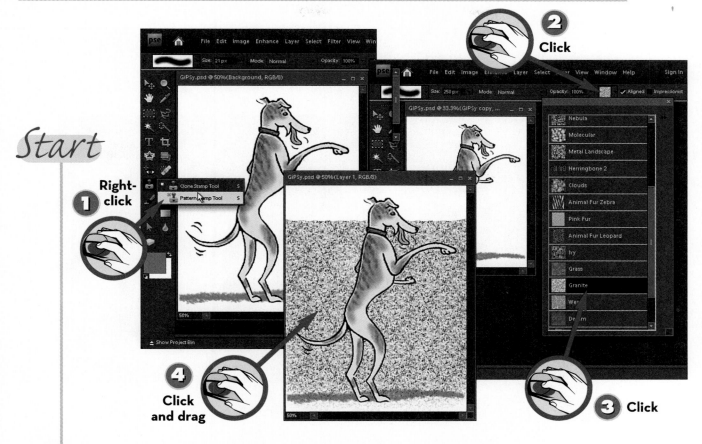

Start

Right-click

1 Click

2 Click

4 Click and drag

3 Click

End

1 Right-click the **Stamp** tool and choose **Pattern Stamp Tool**.

2 Click the pattern swatch to open the **Pattern** menu in the options bar.

3 Click to choose a pattern from the Pattern pop-up menu.

4 Click and drag in the image area to paint, just as you would with the Brush tool.

 NOTE
The Other Stamp Tool
The Pattern Stamp's roommate in the toolbar, the Clone Stamp, isn't so much for painting as it is a tool for removing unwanted details, such as facial blemishes, from photos.

 NOTE
Options, Options
Notice that the options bar contains all kinds of choices. Make your selections before doing step 2, just as you would with a brush.

ERASING PART OF THE IMAGE

The Eraser tool works just like a brush—but removes pixels in its path instead of depositing them. It affects shapes on the currently selected layer only, so you might want to open the Layers palette first to get your bearings.

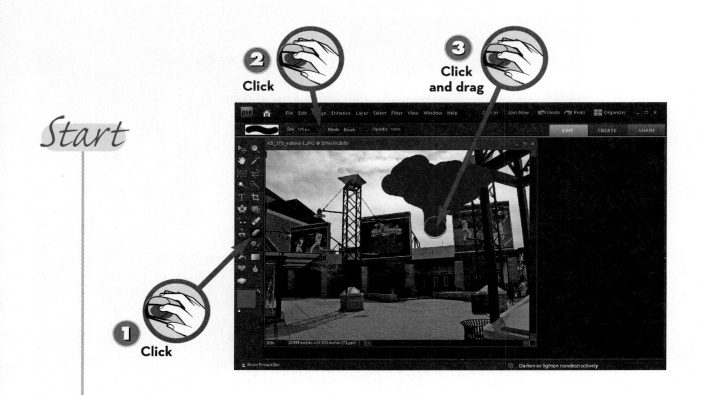

Start

End

1 Switch to the **Eraser** tool, or press **E**.

2 If you want, change the tool properties in the options bar.

3 Click and drag over the pixels you want to erase.

 TIP

Undo Instead?

Use the Eraser tool to partially erase objects in an image. To simply get rid of painting mistakes, **Edit**, **Undo** may be faster and cleaner.

 TIP

Other Eraser Tools

Right-click in step 1 to choose **Background Eraser**, which deletes a single color sampled from the center of a brush, or **Magic Eraser**, which deletes areas of similar-colored pixels with a click (just as Magic Wand does for selections).

SMUDGING THE "PAINT"

Some of the painting tools can be used either for painting or for retouching details in photos, and the Smudge tool is one of these. Artists who've worked with pastels will be familiar with the technique of rubbing chalk edges to soften them.

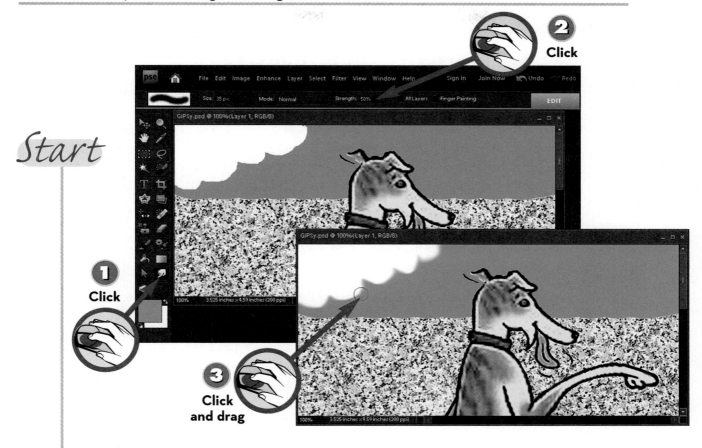

Start

2 Click

1 Click

3 Click and drag

End

1. With the edge you want to soften zoomed in the image area, switch to the **Smudge** tool.

2. If you want, change the tool properties in the options bar.

3. Click and drag along the edge to soften it.

 TIP

Finger Paint, Oh Boy!

If you're tempted to make a creative mess the clean, electronic way, check the **Finger Painting** box in the options bar before you do step 3.

 TIP

Impressionist Brush Instead?

The effect of the Smudge tool may be too subtle for your taste. For more pronounced blurring, use the **Impressionist Brush** tool in one of the smaller brush sizes. Also try effects in the Filter, Blur submenu.

part

FLATTERING YOUR SUBJECTS

In other Parts of this book, we've talked about Photoshop Elements being your photo lab and your art studio—but why not also think of Photoshop Elements as a one-stop health and beauty spa? Digital retouching, if not overdone, can perk up your friends and loved ones, making them appear to shed pounds, revitalizing their complexions, and putting that old sparkle in their eyes—all without risky fad diets, treatments, or pills!

But let's emphasize: Don't overdo it. As a good rule of thumb, try to soften rather than erase. Leave some lines, freckles, and whatever other imperfections give your friend her unique character and winning charm. Go too far, and you'll have a slick beauty shot of a lifeless mannequin.

Many of the techniques described in this Part were applied to the photo on the facing page. Retouching included correcting a color cast, softening facial lines with the Blur tool, removing a mole with the Spot Healing Brush tool, adding eyelight with the Brush tool, lightening shadows and darkening blown-out highlights with the Dodge and Burn tools, and intensifying lip and eye color with the Sponge tool set to Saturate.

The transformation took about 10 minutes—and it makes a lovely person even lovelier.

WHAT A DIFFERENCE A PIXEL MAKES

Before

After

SOFTENING WRINKLES

This one's sure to please—the wrinkle remover. Remember, the lines in the face convey expressiveness, so don't paint them all out. If you do, you'll end up with the face of a plastic fashion doll. Ask yourself: Are these crow's feet or laugh lines?

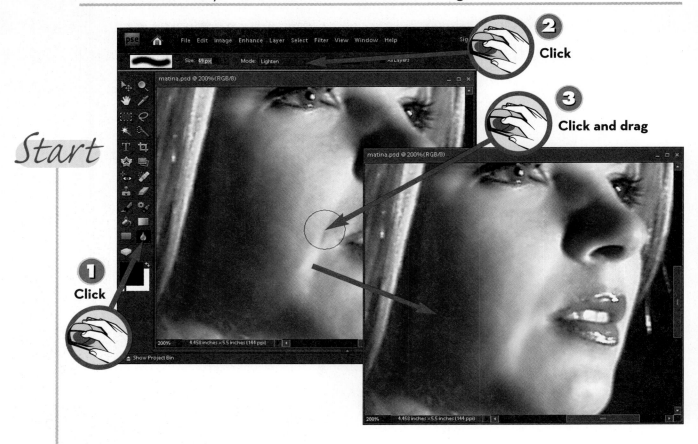

Start

1 Click

2 Click

3 Click and drag

End

1 With a zoomed photo in the Editor's Full Edit mode, switch to the **Blur** tool.

2 In the options bar, choose **Lighten** from the Mode pop-up menu.

3 Click and drag several times over a facial line to blend it away.

NOTE
Mode Options
The Blur tool can be versatile, depending on what you choose in the More Options setting. Besides Normal, Darken, and Lighten (used here), the effect can be confined to Hue, Saturation, Color, Lighter Color, Darker Color, or Luminosity.

TIP
To Be Precise About It
For best results, pick a Soft Round brush tip in the options bar and choose a size just slightly larger than the facial lines you're retouching, and trace along the line as you paint.

REMOVING BLEMISHES

That's right—the Spot Healing Brush tool is a painless zit zapper. But its marvels don't stop there. You can use it to cover up any part of a picture with a texture that Elements creates based on the surrounding pixels. Give it a try to get rid of spots on flower petals, lint on clothes, or any spot you can dab.

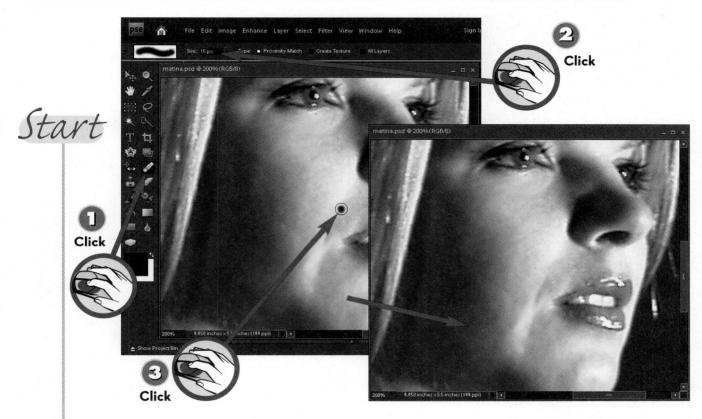

Start

1 Click

2 Click

3 Click

End

1 With a zoomed photo in the Editor's Full Edit mode, switch to the **Spot Healing Brush** tool, or press **J**.

2 Choose a brush size slightly larger than the blemish you want to erase.

3 Click once or twice on the blemish to remove it.

NOTE

The Big Jobs

The Spot Healing Brush works best on, well, spots! Use it to retouch small, "clickable" objects surrounded by relatively clear, flat areas of color, such as moles, pimples, and dust motes. Often, you'll want to retouch larger areas and objects that are right next to other objects you don't want to affect, such as tattoos and smudges. For these jobs, try using the Healing Brush tool instead. Turn to "Painting Problem Areas Away," later in this Part, to learn more.

CHANGING HAIR COLOR

Being able to digitally recolor hair opens up all kinds of possibilities. Try on new looks and print them out to show the colorist at your hair salon. Change your Web photo because an ardent admirer has a thing for redheads. Or go blue, pink, or green without fear of social stigma.

Start

2 Click and drag

3 Click

1 Click

① Switch to the **Quick Selection** tool, or press **A**.

② Click and drag carefully to select the hair.

③ Choose **Layer, New Adjustment Layer, Hue/Saturation**.

Continued

NOTE

It's a Cake, It's a Sandwich

Part 6 discusses layers in more detail, but in these steps you're creating a special layer to contain just the Hue/Saturation effect. This adjustment layer doesn't contain any part of the image. By selecting the area you want to modify before creating the adjustment layer, you restrict its effects to that area.

4 Click **OK**.

5 Adjust the sliders to change the hair color.

6 Click **OK**.

End

-TIP-

Want Subtler Color?

To soften the effect of the Hue/Saturation layer on the underlying hair color, decrease the Opacity value for the new layer in the Layers palette.

-NOTE-

Keep Those Layers

To keep a version of the image that contains editable layers, save your file as a Photoshop (PSD) file.

PAINTING PROBLEM AREAS AWAY

Unlike the Spot Healing Brush, the Healing Brush tool requires you to paint back and forth across whatever you're trying to remove from the image. It's a better bet for fixing larger objects or areas that aren't completely surrounded by the same color or texture, such as tattoos, stray strands of hair, or distracting jewelry.

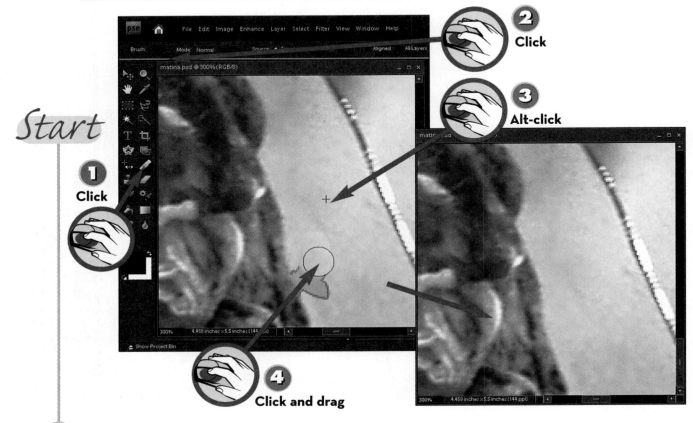

Start

End

1. With a zoomed photo in the Editor's Full Edit mode, switch to the **Healing Brush** tool.

2. Choose a brush size somewhat smaller than the area you want to fill in (in this case a tattoo).

3. **Alt-click** in a clear area of skin to choose a source for the new pixels.

4. Click and drag across the area to paint it with texture copied from the source area.

TIP

Odds Are It'll Be Even

You can use the Healing Brush to even out skin tones. **Alt-click** to place your source point in the area whose color you want to reproduce; choose **Color** from the Mode pop-up menu on the options bar.

ENHANCING OR TONING DOWN A COLOR

The Sponge tool doesn't actually change the color of a selection, it just intensifies (saturates) or reduces (desaturates) it. It comes in handy for brightening up a wardrobe, such as neck scarves, or for toning down a too colorful background that's competing with your subject.

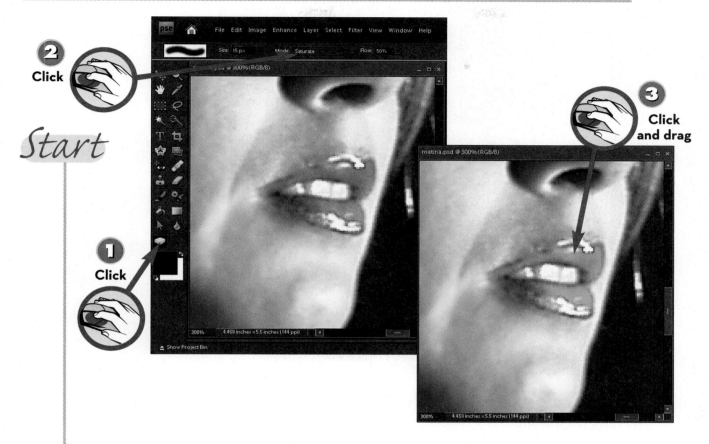

Start

2 Click

3 Click and drag

1 Click

1 With a photo in the active image area, switch to the **Sponge** tool, or press **O**.

2 To enhance color, switch to **Saturate** from the Mode pop-up menu in the options bar.

3 Click and drag over an area to heighten its color.

End

 TIP
Sponge Options
As do many other tools, the options bar offers a selection of brush tip sizes. The Flow setting controls the rate at which pixels become saturated or desaturated as you paint over them.

TIP
Dishwater Results?
If you overuse the Sponge in Desaturate mode, you'll remove all color from the area. That's fine if you're going for a selective monochrome look—or to make skin look downright ghostly.

TRIMMING CONTOURS ON THE FACE OR BODY

We all have an unsightly bulge or two we wouldn't mind getting rid of, right? Well, forget diet and exercise. With the Liquify filter, you can push that saggy skin right where you'd like it to be. No muss, no fuss!

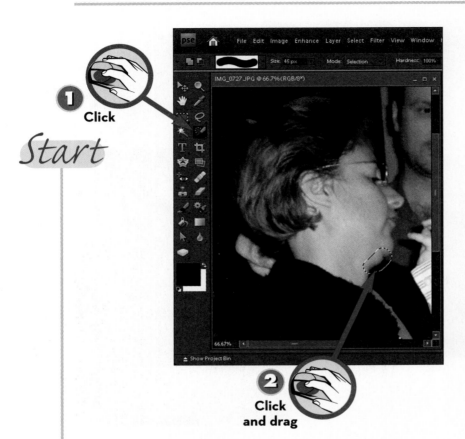

Click

Start

Click and drag

Click

1 Switch to the **Selection Brush** tool or press **A**.

2 Paint a selection around the contour to be reduced; make the inner edge of the selection along the line you want the contour to follow.

3 Choose **Filter**, **Distort**, **Liquify**.

Continued

TIP

Surgical Technique

The trick here is to choose an area that includes either side of an edge, such as a jaw or waistline, and then move it inward—toward the center of the face or body.

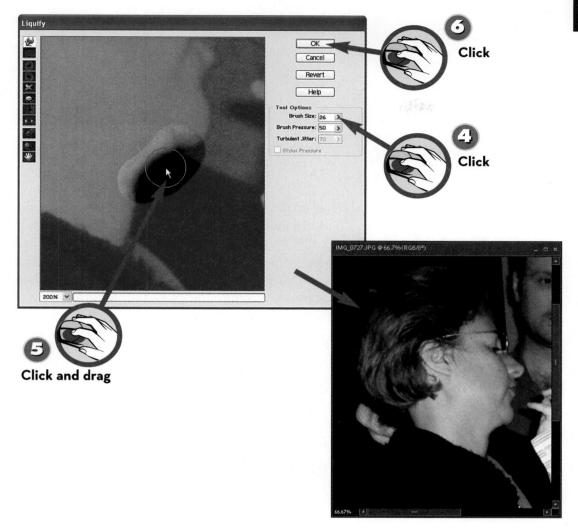

 4 Choose a brush one third to one half the size of the area you want to "tuck."

5 Click and drag toward the inner edge of the selection to reposition the skin.

6 Click **OK**.

End

TIP
Move by Itty Bits
Take it slow and easy when using the Liquify tool. The smaller your movements with the mouse, the more subtle the effect will be. Watch out for adjacent objects—try to drag so that they won't be distorted.

 NOTE
Tidy Up
For a seamless operation, you might need to use other retouching tools, such as Smudge or Clone Stamp, to clean up the edges.

ORGANIZING AND PRESENTING YOUR PHOTOS

Knowing how to crop, clean up, and print your photos is all very well and good—unless you can't find the images you want when you need them. That's what Organizer is all about. It's Photoshop Elements' "other half," the half that keeps track of what and where things are. You can use Organizer to catalog your photos and assign them categories and keywords, and it automatically places all your images in a timeline so that you can easily locate the photos you know you took at last year's Fourth of July party.

Organizer has hidden depths, too: It's also a creative hub where you can turn your photos into slide shows, themed scrapbook pages, Web photo galleries, or even personalized, one-of-a-kind hardbound books. After all, the whole point of taking wonderful photos is to be able to share them, right?

Organizer can recognize faces all by itself, so you can have it show you all the photos in your collection that include people. This makes for much faster tagging (tags are what Organizer calls categories). You can even assign photos to locations on a map, so you'll be able to locate all the images in your collection that were taken at your favorite vacation destination or at any other specific place.

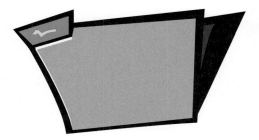

THANKS FOR THE MEMORIES

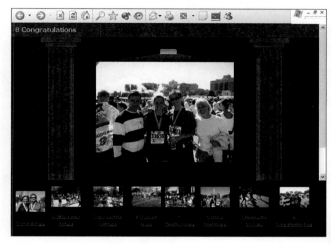

Web Photo Gallery

Slide Show

Album Pages

CREATING AN ALBUM

Organizer is very good at finding the photos you're looking for, but sometimes it's more efficient to group related images together ahead of time, so you can display them all with a single click. These collections of pictures are called albums, and you can create as many as you want.

Start

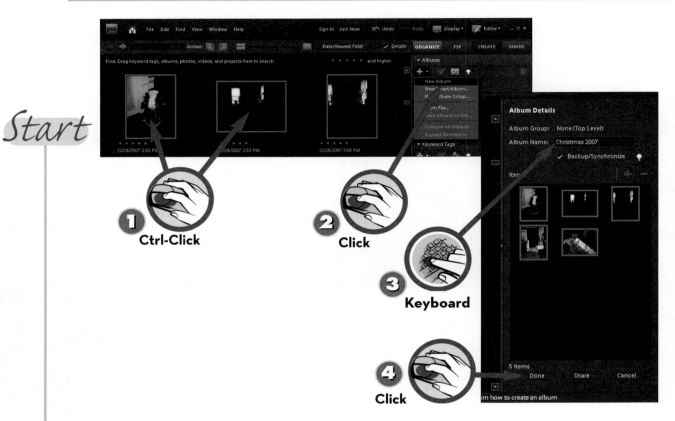

Ctrl-Click

Click

Keyboard

Click

1. In the Organizer's Organize mode, Ctrl-click to select the photos you want to include in the new album.

2. Click the **Create New Album** button at the top of the Album palette and choose **New Album**.

3. Enter a name for the album.

4. Click **Done**.

End

TIP
Ch-ch-ch-changes
To change the name or attributes of an album after you've created it, click its name in the Albums palette and then click the **Edit** button just to the right of the New Album button at the top of the Albums palette.

NOTE
How Will I Know?
Organizer indicates that a photo belongs to an album by placing a small icon resembling a physical photo album below the picture. The icon's color lets you know which album the photo is part of.

ASSIGNING KEYWORDS TO PHOTOS

Keyword tags enable you to locate photos by assigning them categories. For example, you could apply the Family keyword tag to all the images that contain pictures of your family members. Then, viewing those photos (and excluding all the lovely but boring landscape images from your vacation) can be accomplished with a single click.

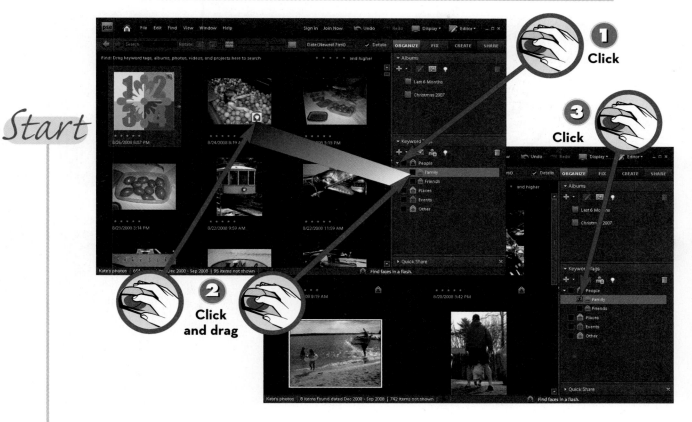

Start

End

1. Click the triangle next to a keyword tag category to reveal the tags it contains.

2. Click a keyword tag and drag it to a photo to apply it to that image.

3. To view all photos tagged with a keyword, check the box next to that tag in the Keyword Tags palette.

-TIP-
Tag Sale
Tags are free—make as many as you need to satisfy your sense of order. Click the **Create New Keyword Tag** button at the top of the palette and choose **New Keyword Tag** to create your own tags. For example, you might make a tag for club activities and one for vacations.

-TIP-
Batch Tagging
You can assign a tag to more than one photo at a time. **Shift-click** to select the photos you want to tag, and then drag the tag onto any one of them. The tag is assigned to all the selected pictures.

FINDING PHOTOS IN ORGANIZER

Organizer provides several ways to locate your photos, including searching by date, by keyword tag, or by visual similarity. This task shows you a few ways to look for photos you can't seem to locate.

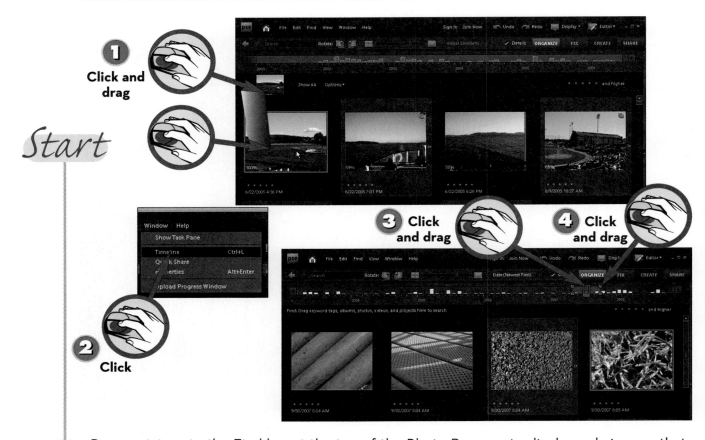

Start

① Click and drag

② Click

③ Click and drag

④ Click and drag

① Drag a picture to the Find bar at the top of the Photo Browser to display only images that are visually similar to that picture.

② If you don't see the timeline at the top of the Photo Browser, choose **Window, Timeline**.

③ Drag the **date marker** to view photos taken on the corresponding date on the timeline.

④ Drag the **endpoint markers** at the ends of the timeline to narrow down the range of photos shown.

Continued

-TIP-

Second Date

You can also look at a Calendar view of your photos, with the photos for each day stacked up on that box of the calendar page. Choose **Display, Date View** at the top of the Organizer window, or press **Ctrl+Alt+D**.

-NOTE-

A Very Long Timeline

If your timeline doesn't all show at the top of the Photo Browser, click the arrows at either end to scroll through its entire length.

5. Drag a keyword tag to the Find bar to display all the images tagged with that keyword.

6. Drag another keyword tag to the Find bar to display only images tagged with both keywords.

7. Choose **Options, Show Results That Do Not Match** to see the pictures that don't use either of those keywords.

8. Click **Show All** to display all the images in your photo catalog.

End

TIP
More Than Meets the Eye
Show Results That Do Not Match in the Find bar's Options pop-up menu may be a more useful command than you think. For example, if you use Photoshop Elements' face-recognition feature to tag images that contain people (turn to the next task, "Tagging Pictures of People Automatically," to learn how), you can easily locate all the pictures that *don't* contain people, making it quicker to find landscapes, still lifes, and animal photos.

TAGGING PICTURES OF PEOPLE AUTOMATICALLY

Tagging your photos is an important part of getting them organized, but it's a lot of work. Elements can help out by finding people's faces wherever they show up in your photos and presenting them to you in a single window so that you can tag photos of people efficiently.

Start

1 Click

2 Click

3 Click and drag

1 Choose **Find, Find Faces for Tagging**.

2 Click **Yes**.

3 After Photoshop Elements finds all the faces, drag the appropriate keyword tag to each photo to apply it to that image.

End

 NOTE
Your Choice
Don't forget, you can create as many tags as you like. You might want to tag photos with people's names, or perhaps you prefer a more streamlined approach and want to use just "Friends" and "Family." It's up to you!

NOTE
Show Me
Click **Show Already Tagged Faces** at the top of the Find Faces window if you want to see all the faces, even the ones you've already tagged. When this box isn't checked, Elements hides photos as soon as you tag them.

RATING YOUR PICTURES

Of course, parents and teachers aren't supposed to play favorites, but it's perfectly all right for photographers to do so. In Photoshop Elements, you can assign each picture a rating in stars (just like the movies) from 0 to 5. This provides yet another way to find specific photos when you want them.

Start

1 Click

2 Click

3 Click

4 Click

1 Click a photo in the Photo Browser.

2 Click a star below the image's thumbnail to assign it a rating.

3 Click a star at the top of the Photo Browser to show only photos that match the specified rating.

4 Choose **And Higher**, **And Lower**, or **Only**.

End

TIP
It Thrills Me, It Thrills Me Not
Change a photo's rating at any time by just clicking a different star below the image's thumbnail.

NOTE
Rated Five for Fabulous
You don't have to give each of your pictures a star rating; I tend to save this feature for pictures that I particularly like. Five-star photos are my all-time favorites, four-star images are suitable for publication, and so on.

PUTTING PICTURES ON THE MAP

We've seen that Photoshop Elements knows about time (as in the timeline and the Date view); amazingly, it also knows about space. Not outer space, but space as in location. Via the program's connection to Yahoo! Maps, you can assign a map location to any photo or to a keyword tag.

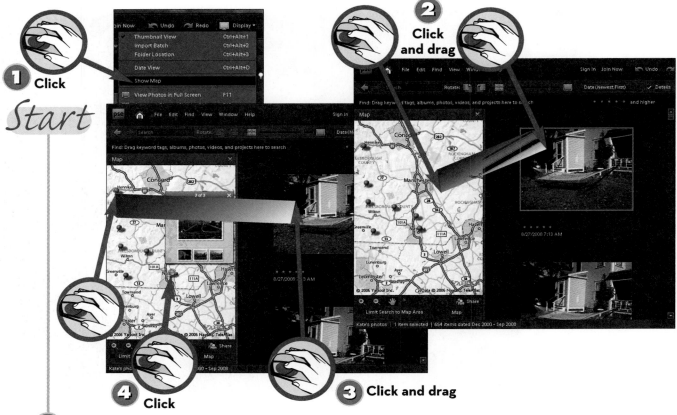

Start

1 Click

2 Click and drag

3 Click and drag

4 Click

1. Choose **Display**, **Show Map**.

2. Click a photo and drag it onto the map to create a new location.

3. Drag a photo to a red map pin to assign it an existing location.

4. To see the photos associated with a location, switch to the Hand tool and click the red map pin at that location.

End

NOTE

Once Is Enough

The first time you click Show Map, you'll see a dialog explaining the different ways you can use the Map view. Read through it, and then check the box labeled **Don't Show Again** so that you don't have to deal with this dialog every time you use the map.

COLLECTING PHOTOS INTO STACKS

As your photo collection grows larger, you may find that you want to consolidate similar photos in the Photo Browser. The Organizer provides a simple way to do that: Stack them up. Stacking makes your Browser more useful because you can see more different photos at one time, rather than several very similar images.

Start

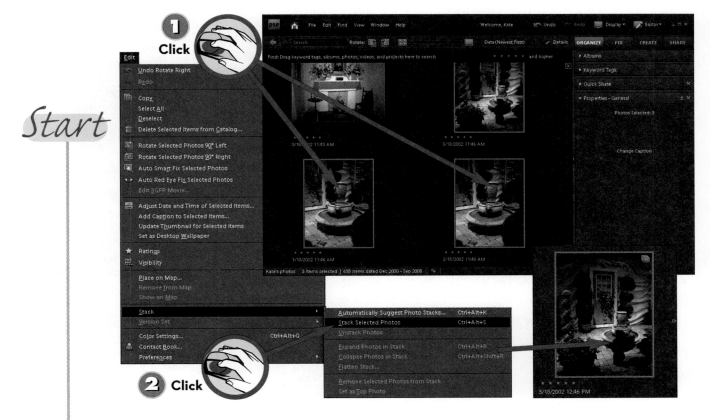

1 Click

2 Click

1 **Ctrl-click** to select the photos you want to stack.

2 Choose **Edit**, **Stack**, **Stack Selected Photos**.

End

TIP

Hurry Up!
The quickest way to hide and show the photos in a stack is to click the arrow to its right in the Photo Browser.

TIP

Shuffling the Stack
To choose which photo shows on top of the stack in the Photo Browser, choose **Edit**, **Stack**, **Expand Photos in Stack**. Click the one you want to use, and then choose **Edit**, **Stack**, **Set as Top Photo**.

CREATING A SMART ALBUM

If you find yourself performing the same search in the Organizer more than once, stop right there. It's time to create a smart album, one that remembers search criteria rather than specific images, and updates itself every time you add photos to your catalog, or remove them. You can base a smart album on any kind of search criteria at all.

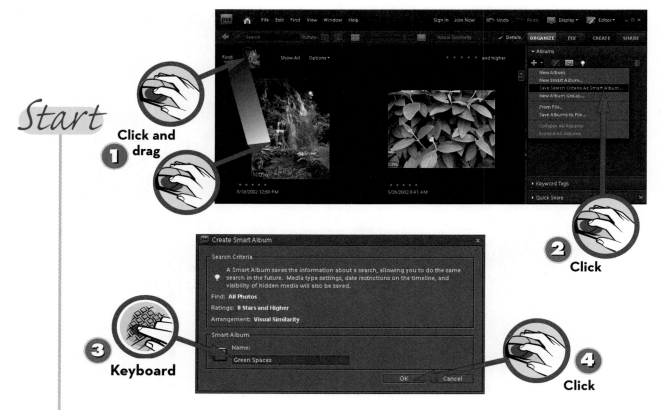

Start

Click and drag 1

2 **Click**

3 **Keyboard**

4 **Click**

1 Drag an image to the Find bar and enter any search criteria to search for images to include in the smart album.

2 Click the **Create New Album** button at the top of the Albums palette and choose **Save Search Criteria as Smart Album**.

3 Enter a name for the album.

4 Click **OK** to create the new smart album.

Continued

TIP

Changed Your Mind?

To change the search criteria associated with an existing smart album, first perform the search using the criteria you want to assign to the album, then right-click the album's name in the Albums palette and choose **Save Current Search to *YourAlbumName* Album**.

NOTE

A Law Unto Themselves

Smart albums are so smart that they don't allow you to change their contents unless you change their search criteria. You can't add a photo to a smart album manually, remove one manually, or reorder the images.

Click 6

Click 5

 5 Click the album's name in the Albums palette to instantly perform the same search at any time.

6 Click the **Edit Album** button at the top of the Albums palette to change its name.

End

TIP

Nitty Gritty

If you really want to dig down into the details to search for images in a smart album, start by choosing **Find**, **By Details (Metadata)**. In the dialog, choose the search criteria for the smart album. Click the plus sign (+) to add a criterion or the minus sign (–) to remove one. You can search based on 30 different criteria, including the camera make and model, the image's location on the map, and even whether it's horizontally or vertically oriented.

MANAGING YOUR CATALOG ON PHOTOSHOP.COM

Photoshop.com is Adobe's free photo-sharing service, which ties neatly into Photoshop Elements itself. You can use Photoshop.com to share photos with friends, to add photos to your catalog from anywhere, to back up your albums, and more. First, though, you have to sign up for a free membership and upload your images.

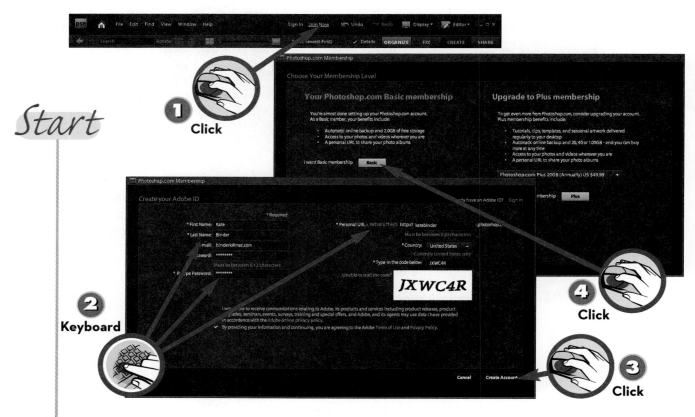

Start

1 Click

2 Keyboard

3 Click

4 Click

1 At the top of the Organizer window, click **Join Now** to establish a Photoshop.com account.

2 In the dialog, enter the requested information and choose a personal URL for your Photoshop.com subsite.

3 Click **Create Account**.

4 Click **Basic** to choose a free membership.

Continued

TIP

It Works Like This

To share images between your Photoshop Elements catalog and Photoshop.com, they must be part of an album (not a smart album) that's set to be synchronized.

NOTE

The Shortest Route

You don't have to start Photoshop Elements up completely to change your Photoshop.com preferences. You can access your Photoshop.com site and change backup and synchronization settings via the Welcome screen.

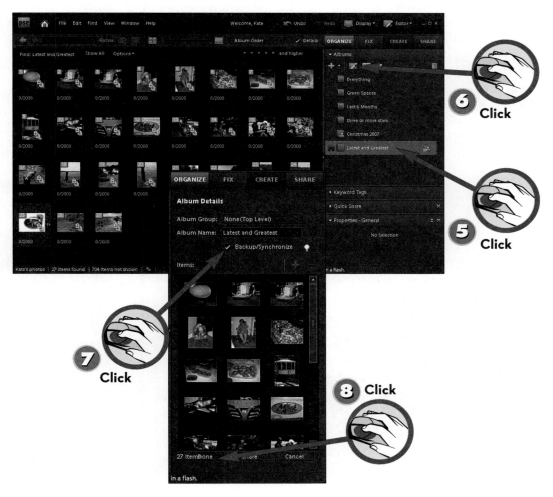

5 To add an album to your online collection, click its name in the Albums palette.

6 Click the **Edit Album** button.

7 Check the box marked **Backup/Synchronize**.

8 Click **Done**.

End

NOTE

Having Trouble?

If your Photoshop.com site doesn't contain the photos you've marked for synchronization in Photoshop Elements, check the Photoshop Elements preferences (choose **Edit**, **Preferences**, **Backup/Synchronization**) to be sure that there's a check in the box marked **Backup/Sync Is On**.

ADDING IMAGES VIA PHOTOSHOP.COM

Don't wait until you get home from your vacation to add your latest photos to your collection; upload them to Photoshop.com and stop worrying about lost or damaged media. Once pictures are on Photoshop.com, too, you can share them starting right away, instead of waiting. (See the next task for instructions.)

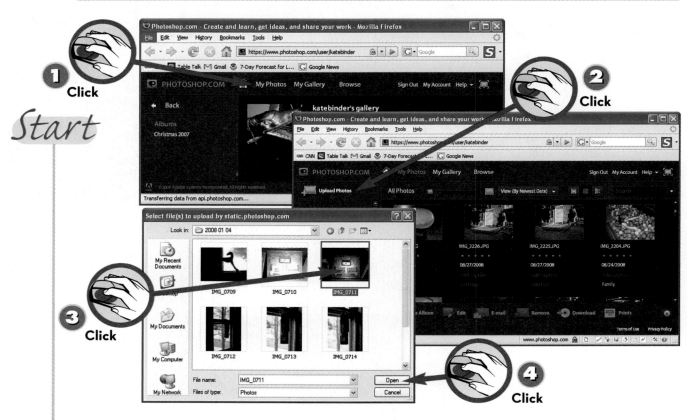

Start

1 Click

2 Click

3 Click

4 Click

1 Go to the custom URL you chose when you signed up and click **My Photos** to see your collection.

2 Click **Upload Photos** to add new images.

3 Click the name of the file you want to upload.

4 Click **Open**.

End

TIP
How Refreshing
When images are uploading, or Photoshop Elements is syncing an album, you can click the Refresh button at the right end of the Photoshop.com toolbar to update your view of the images in your catalog.

NOTE
One Chance to Get It Right
After you've created your account, you can't change your personal URL, so choose wisely. You can, however, update your name, email address, and password by clicking My Account at the top of the Photoshop.com window.

WORKING WITH YOUR ONLINE COLLECTION

You don't have to take your computer with you to edit and share the photos in your collection. If you're signed up with a Photoshop.com account, you can print, email, share, or even edit (using Photoshop Express) your pictures on any computer with a Web connection.

Start

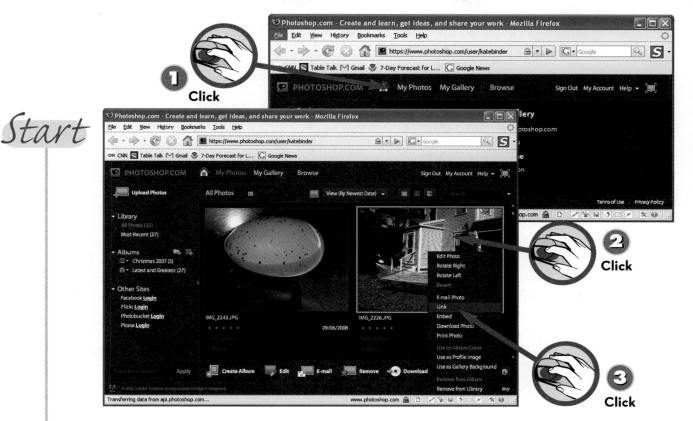

Click

Click

Click

1. Go to the custom URL you chose when you signed up and click **My Photos** to see your collection.

2. Click a photo's thumbnail to work with it.

3. Click **Photo Options** and choose a command from the pop-up menu.

End

NOTE
Don't Be Afraid to Delete
When you edit or delete a photo from your library on Photoshop.com, Photoshop Elements doesn't delete the original version of that image from its own catalog. Instead, it creates a version set that contains both the original and the modified version.

NOTE
Universal Access
Don't forget that to have access to your images in Photoshop.com, including editing them using Photoshop Express, you'll need to set your albums to synchronize in Photoshop Elements.

PUBLISHING YOUR IMAGES

Maybe you're about to enter the big world of publishing, whether print or online. Or maybe you just want to get your images out into the wide world so that folks can see them. Either way, the tasks in this Part will set you on your way.

We'll start out by looking at ways to apply the same fixes to a whole batch of images at once, so that you can get them ready to appear in your magnum opus. Then, you'll learn how to save an image in the right format, size, and resolution for use on a Website.

Next we'll move on to some of the many exciting projects Photoshop Elements can help you create, from printable album pages for your scrapbook to a gorgeous animated Web photo gallery. You can create a slide show, order traditional photo prints all the way up to poster size, or create a classy hardbound photo book. To get started with any of these projects, you can choose photos individually from your collection or use an existing album. (To review ways to organize your photo collection into albums, flip back to Part 10, "Organizing and Presenting Your Photos.)

There's not enough room in this book to cover all the projects you can create with Photoshop Elements, such as customized CD covers and photo calendars. But in this Part, you'll get a taste of what's possible and see how the program works through these projects in general. From there, the sky's the limit!

GETTING THEM OUT THERE

We all love to show off our latest pictures. Whether online...

...or in print, Photoshop Elements can make your photos look even better than they already do.

FIXING MULTIPLE IMAGES

Have a bunch of pictures that need fixing? You can have Photoshop Elements do the work while you refill your coffee cup. Enjoy a break while Elements adjusts the lighting, color, and sharpness of your images; resizes them; renames them; and saves them in your preferred format.

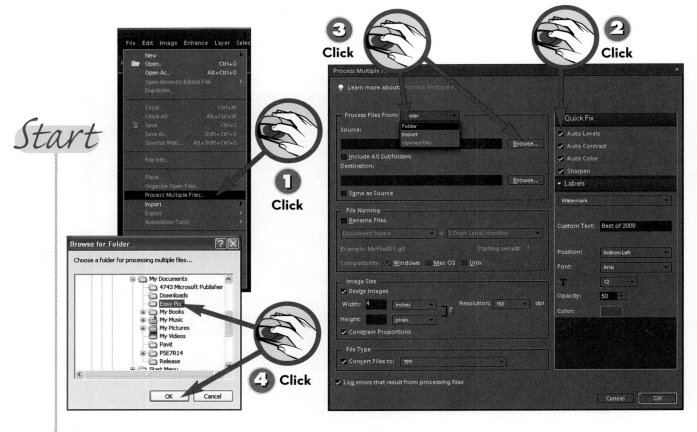

Start

1. In the Editor's Full Edit mode, choose **File**, **Process Multiple Files**.

2. Choose the **Quick Fix** operations you want to apply.

3. Choose **Folder** from the Process Files From pop-up menu, and then click **Browse**.

4. Navigate to the folder of images you want to process, and then click **OK**.

Continued

TIP
Get Organized First
Be sure to put all the image files you want to process in a single folder, so that Elements will be able to work with them all at one time.

NOTE
You Have a Choice
After step 4, you get to choose a place for the revised files to be saved. Either click **Browse** to pick a destination folder, or check **Save as Source**.

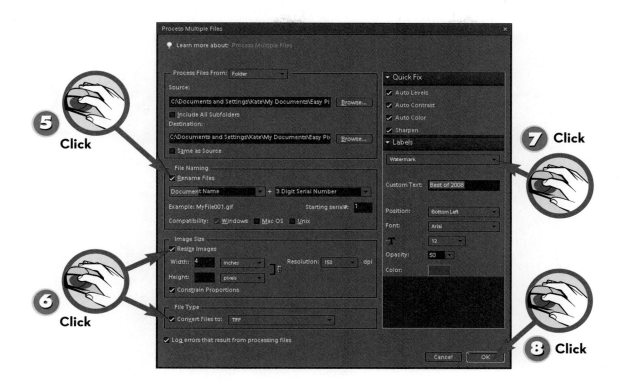

⑤ Click

⑥ Click

⑦ Click

⑧ Click

⑤ Choose **Rename Files** to automatically give the files consistent names.

⑥ Choose **Resize Images** and **Convert Files To** if you want to resize the images and save them in a different format.

⑦ Choose **Watermark** in the Labels section to add overlaid labels to the images.

⑧ Click **OK** to begin processing.

End

TIP
What's a Watermark?
A *watermark* is a semitransparent design or line of text overlaid on an image to identify it. It's a great way to ensure everyone knows your pictures are yours, without obscuring their details.

CAUTION
Be Careful
Don't choose **Same as Source** under **Destination** unless you don't want to keep your original files. With this option turned on, Elements overwrites the originals with the revised versions. But it warns you first with a dialog, so you can change the setting if you want.

OPTIMIZING A PICTURE FOR THE WEB

Preparing an image for the Web involves converting its file type to JPEG, GIF, or PNG; restricting its colors to 256; (usually) reducing its size to a few inches wide; and limiting its resolution to 72 pixels/inch.

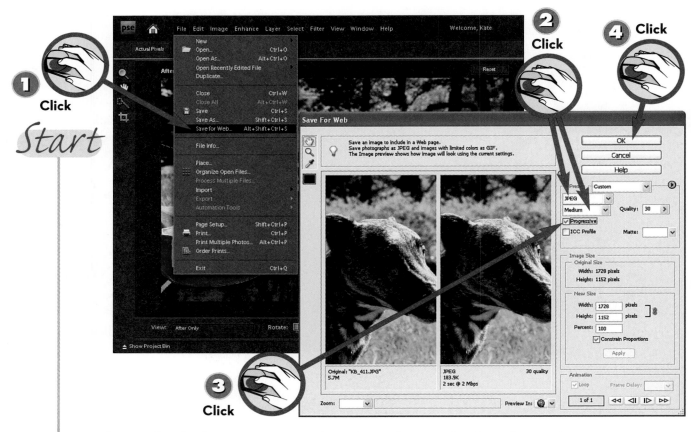

Click

Start

Click

Click

Click

Click

1. With your finished picture open in the Editor, choose **File**, **Save for Web** (**Alt+Shift+Ctrl+S**).

2. In the Preset area, choose a picture format and quality, such as JPEG Medium.

3. Optionally, check the **Progressive** box (see note at the bottom of the page).

4. Click **OK**.

Continued

TIP

Progressive Mode

Choosing Progressive mode for a JPEG file causes it to display in stages as it downloads, resulting in a more pleasing experience for users with relatively slow (dial-up) connections.

5 Click

5 Click **Save**.

End

TIP

Control File Size

You can choose **Image, Resize, Image Size** before saving to size the image appropriately for a Web page; most Web images are 2 to 4 inches wide, with a resolution of 72 pixels/inch.

TIP

Control Image Size

To capture the interest of Web surfers, you want your home page to load as quickly as possible. Keep the images shown there at thumbnail size, but permit interested viewers to click them to download higher-resolution pictures.

BUILDING PRINTABLE ALBUM PAGES

Having all your pictures on your computer is very convenient, but lots of times you still want to look at those pictures on paper, in a photo album or scrapbook. Whether your style is traditional (black photo corners on plain pages) or modern (scrapbook designs of every type imaginable), you'll find a template and layout option to suit you in Photoshop Elements' Photo Collage Wizard.

Ctrl-click

1

2

Click

Start

3

Click

1 In the Organizer, Ctrl-click to select the photos you want to include in your printed album pages.

2 Click the **Create** button.

3 Click **Photo Collage**.

Continued

TIP

Pages or a Book?

Album pages are great for adding to your real-life photo albums or scrapbooks; you can also frame them for a nice gift for grandparents and family friends. If you'd like to create something a little fancier, turn to "Creating a Photo Book," later in this Part.

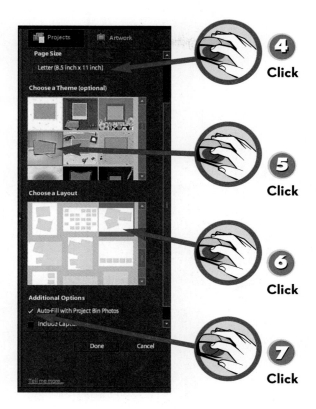

4 Click

5 Click

6 Click

7 Click

4 Choose a paper size from the Page Size pop-up menu.

5 Choose a theme from the 48 built-in choices.

6 Choose a layout for your page based on the number of images it will contain.

7 Uncheck the **Auto-Fill with Project Bin Photos** box.

Continued

TIP
Moving Day
You can move photos around within their frames, and you can move the frames so that they don't overlap important areas of other images. Just click and drag after the photos have been dropped in.

NOTE
Too Same-y?
Each page in a Photo Collage project uses the same layout. If you want to produce multiple pages with different layouts, you have two choices. You can either create a photo book or create a separate photo collage for each page.

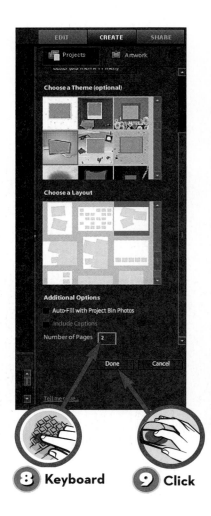

8 Keyboard

9 Click

10 Click and drag

11 Click

8 Enter the number of pages you're creating; all pages will have the same layout and theme.

9 Click **Done**.

10 Click and drag each photo from the Project Bin to a slot on the page.

11 Click the **Rotate** button or drag the slider to resize a photo.

Continued

 TIP

Automatic Scrapbooking

When you're in a hurry, leave the **Auto-Fill with Project Bin Photos** box checked; then Photoshop Elements will drop your photos into the page layout in the order in which they appear in the Project Bin.

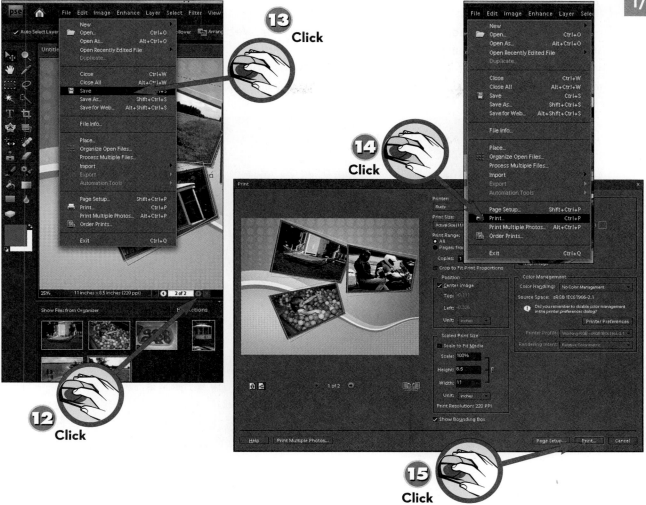

12 Click the **Next Page** button to move to the next page.

13 When you have finished adding pictures, choose **File**, **Save**.

14 Choose **File**, **Print**.

15 Click **Print**.

End

NOTE

Adding Captions

If you want to add captions to your images, you need to do two things: Enter the caption information ahead of time and check the **Include Captions** box. To attach a caption to an image, click the photo in the Organizer and choose **Window**, **Properties**, and then type in the **Caption** field.

MAKING A WEB PHOTO GALLERY

Photoshop Elements includes a variety of designs for Web pages, and the program can automatically insert your photos and descriptive text into its templates with just a few clicks. It then generates completed pages ready for uploading to your own Website, exports them to a CD or DVD, or automatically sends the gallery to Photoshop.com.

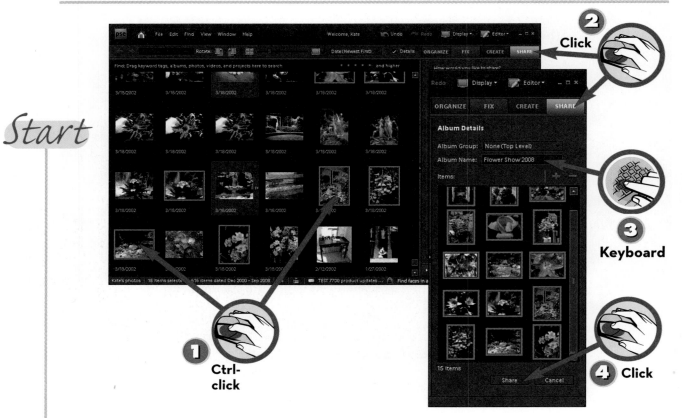

Start

2 Click

3 Keyboard

1 Ctrl-click

4 Click

1 In the Organizer, **Ctrl-click** to select the photos you want to include in your Web gallery.

2 Click **Share**, and then click **Online Album**.

3 Enter a name for the album.

4 Click **Share**.

Continued

TIP

Where's That Picture?

If you realize just as you're getting started setting options for your Web gallery that you've left out your favorite photo, click the **Add** button (+) in the Items section any time before step 4 to return to the Organizer and select it.

5 Click **Change Template**.

6 Click a template.

7 Click **Apply**.

8 Click **Next**.

Continued

TIP

What Is That Again?

If you haven't entered any captions for your photos in the Organizer's Properties palette, Photoshop Elements won't insert any text on the album pages. To store caption information with your photos, see "Adding and Printing Photo Captions" in Part 5.

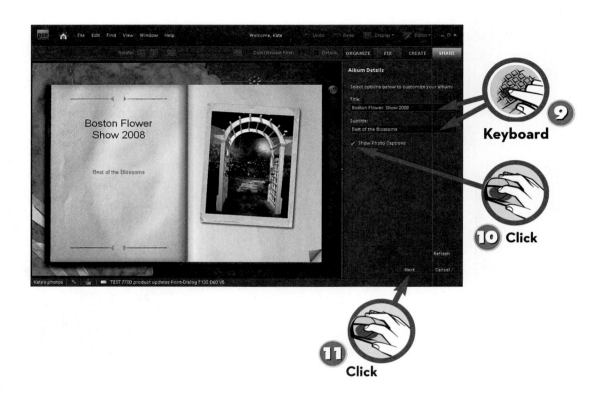

9 Enter a title and a subtitle for the album.

10 Check or uncheck the **Show Photo Captions** box, depending on whether you want to include text captions in the album.

11 Click **Next**.

Continued

NOTE

Oops!

If you don't enter a folder name in the Destination area before clicking **Export** in step 15, Elements reminds you politely to do so. This name is assigned to the folder that Elements creates to hold all the HTML and image files that make up the gallery. To upload the finished gallery to your Website, just upload the entire folder with all its contents.

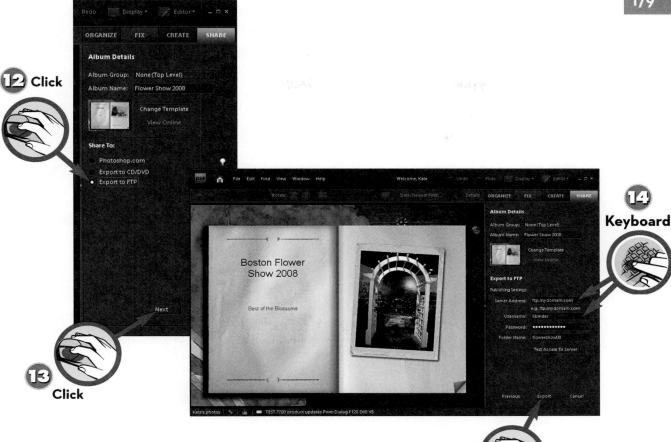

14 Keyboard

13 Click

15 Click

12 Choose an export option.

13 Click **Next**.

14 Enter the appropriate settings for your choice of export method.

15 Click **Export** (for FTP or CD/DVD) or **Share** (for Photoshop.com).

End

NOTE

What Settings?

The information you'll need to supply in step 14 varies depending on which choice you made in step 12. If you're planning to upload the gallery files to a Website via FTP, you must enter your FTP server's address, username, and password. To share your images on Photoshop.com, just choose whether you want to make the album public or share it only with certain friends. Then you enter email addresses and a message for the announcement email. Finally, if you just want to put your gallery on a CD or DVD, choose your CD or DVD drive and give the disc a name.

CREATING A SLIDE SHOW

What better way to get a good look at your photos—and share them with your friends—than to sit back and let them display themselves one at a time? But, this slide show is not your granddad's musty slide carousel and projector with the burnt-out bulb. It's a PDF or a movie file that you can use in many ways.

Ctrl-click

Start

Click

Click

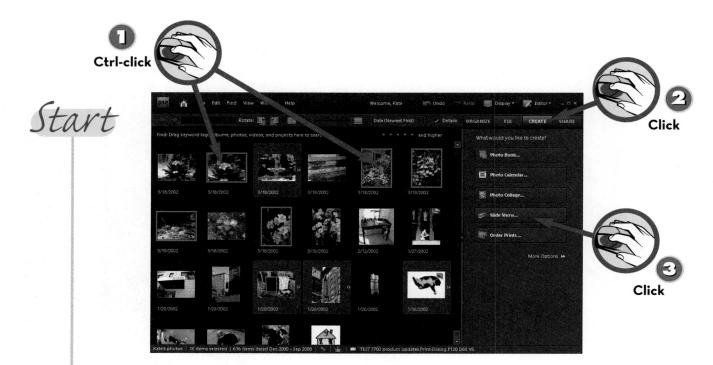

1 In the Organizer, **Ctrl-click** to select the photos you want to include in your slide show.

2 Click **Create**.

3 Click **Slide Show**.

Continued

TIP
Everything in Order
Elements places photos in your show in the order that they occupy in the Photo Browser. To change their order, drag and drop them in the preview area at the bottom of the Slide Show Editor window.

NOTE
Party Favor
Slide shows are fun to play at big events, such as anniversary or milestone birthday parties. Collect photos of the people being honored, choose one of their favorite songs, and go to town! The guests will love it.

4 Click

5 Click

6 Click

7 Drag and drop

4 Set your slide show preferences, such as the duration of each slide and the background color.

5 Click **OK**.

6 Click **Add Blank Slide** to insert a blank slide for your title.

7 Drag and drop slides at the bottom of the window to change their order.

Continued

 TIP

Talking About Photos

If your PC has a microphone, you can record a voiceover track for each slide. Click **Narration** at the top of the Extras palette, and then click the **Record** button to add narration. Click **Stop** when you're done, and click **Play** to play back the recording.

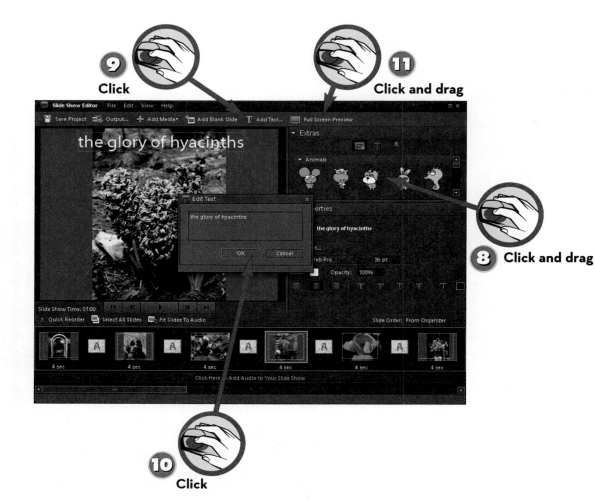

9 Click

11 Click and drag

8 Click and drag

10 Click

8 Drag and drop graphics from the Extras palette onto the slides.

9 Click **Add Text** to insert text on a slide.

10 Enter your text and click **OK**.

11 Click **Full Screen Preview** to see what the slide show will look like.

Continued

 TIP
Taking a Break
If you need to stop working on your slide show before it's finished, click **Save Project** at the top of the Slide Show Editor window to create a project file that you can reopen when you have time to complete the show.

 TIP
PDF or WMV?
A PDF file can be opened in the free Adobe Reader on any computer, but it can't contain special effects such as pan and zoom. To use all the animation bells and whistles, save your slide show as a WMV file.

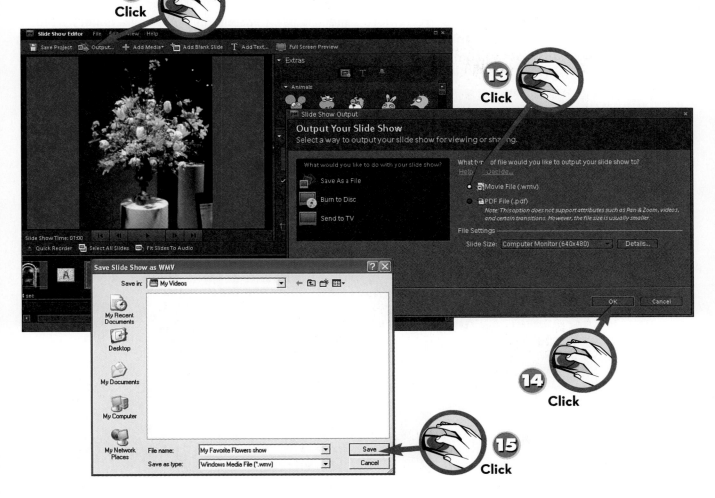

12 Click **Output**.

13 Click **Save as a File** and choose a file type option.

14 Click **OK**.

15 Give the slide show a name and click **Save**.

End

TIP

The Music of the Slides

To add a musical soundtrack, click **Add Media** at the top of the Slide Show Editor window and choose **Audio from Folder**. Choose a music file and click **OK**. Then, to make the slide show the same length as the song, click **Fit Slides to Audio**.

SHARING AN EXISTING ALBUM ONLINE

When you've already collected your photos into albums within Photoshop Elements, the process of turning one into a Web photo gallery is even easier than creating a gallery from scratch. You'll need to sign up for a free Photoshop.com membership. (See "Managing Your Catalog on Photoshop.com," in Part 10, for instructions.) Then, just follow these steps.

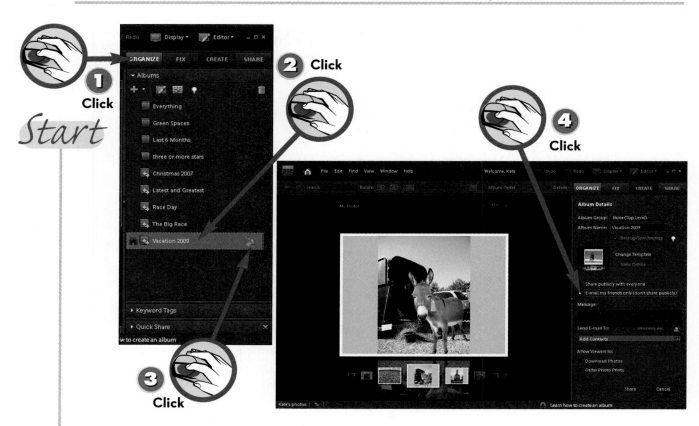

1. In the Organizer, click **Organize**.

2. Click an album in the Albums palette.

3. Click the **Share** button next to the album's name.

4. Choose whether you will make the album public or share it only with friends.

Continued

NOTE
Making It Work
You can only share regular albums; this procedure doesn't work with Smart Albums.

NOTE
How Public Is Public?
Public albums can be browsed by anyone who visits the Photoshop.com Website. Visitors can see your name, address, and other personal data, however, only if you specifically add that information to your online galleries.

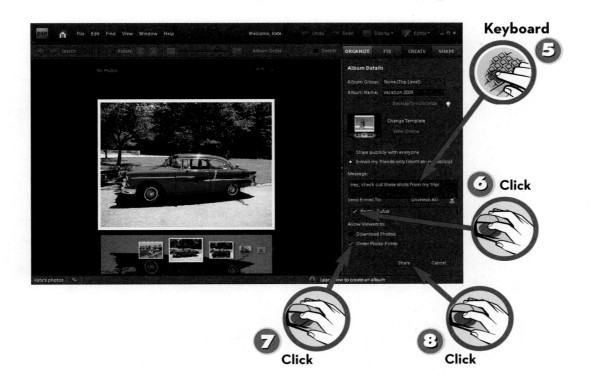

Keyboard **5**

6 **Click**

7 **Click**

8 **Click**

5 If you are sharing the album only with friends, enter a message for the announcement email that Photoshop Elements will send.

6 Click to add your friends' email addresses.

7 Choose whether viewers can download your images and whether they can order prints.

8 Click **Share**.

End

TIP
Keeping in Contact
Photoshop Elements saves the email addresses you enter so that you can reuse them in the future. You can even import addresses from your email program so that you don't have to retype them; just click **Import** in the Contact Book dialog.

ORDERING PRINTS

Want to frame one of your pictures? Want to send prints with your holiday cards? Or, even make a poster to hang on your wall? You can order prints of your photos right from Photoshop Elements, via Kodak's EasyShare Gallery service. It's completely secure, so you don't have to worry about entering your credit card information, and you can have prints shipped to you or pick them up locally.

Start

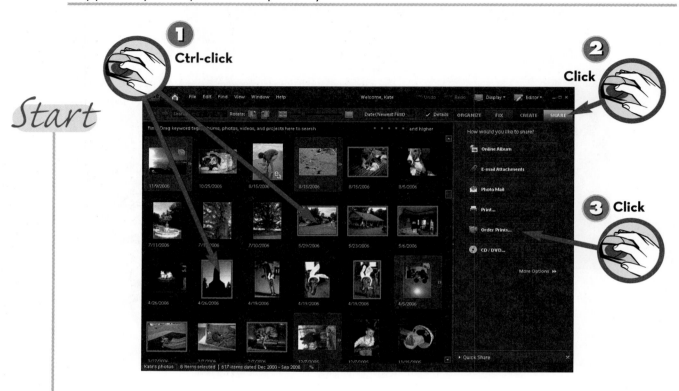

① Ctrl-click

② Click

③ Click

① In the Organizer, **Ctrl-click** to select the photos you want to include in your slide show.

② Click **Share**.

③ Click **Order Prints**.

Continued

 NOTE
Just What You Want
When you're choosing print sizes and quantities, the boxes at the top of the window enable you to order single or double prints of each photo. The box for a single 4 × 6 print of each picture is checked by default.

 NOTE
Watch the Resolution
You can choose different numbers and sizes of prints for each picture. An icon next to each one indicates whether its resolution is high enough. If you see a brown minus sign, reduce the size until the icon turns into a green check mark.

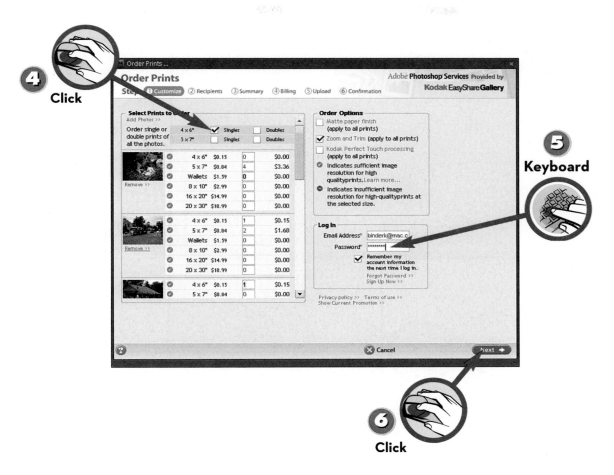

4 Click

5 Keyboard

6 Click

④ Choose the print sizes and quantities that you want to order.

⑤ Enter your username and password (or click **Sign Up Now** if you don't have an account).

⑥ Click **Next**.

Continued

TIP
Think Ahead
If you know you're going to want to order a poster-size print of an image when you're shooting it, be sure to set your camera to its highest resolution. You need a lot of pixels to produce a good image at poster size.

NOTE
First Time for Everything
The first time you log in, you might see a few extra windows asking for your login information. After that, you'll see exactly what you see here each time you use the Order Prints service.

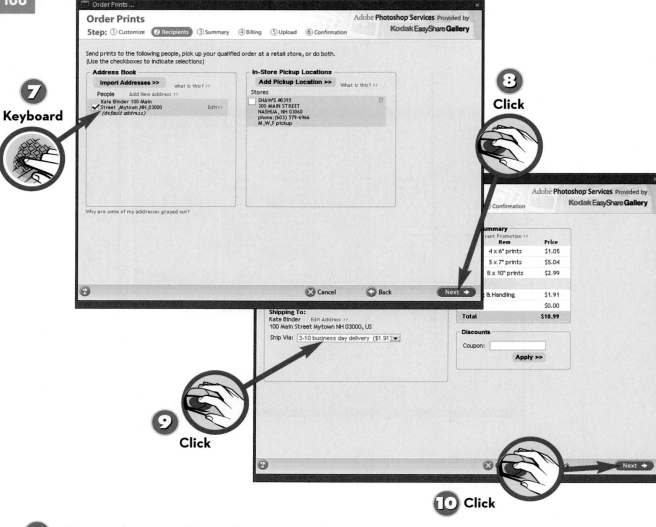

7 Enter a shipping address for prints or choose a pickup location.

8 Click **Next**.

9 Choose a shipping option.

10 Click **Next**.

Continued

TIP

Save Time, Save Money

If you're ordering a set of prints to send to a friend or relative, why not have it shipped directly to that person? You can enter address info for multiple recipients, not just yourself. Photoshop Elements saves this information so that you can use it again and again.

NOTE

Pick Up Where?

The in-store pickup locations are grocery and drug-store chains such as Kmart and Kroger. There's no shipping charge if you pick up your photos locally, but you will pay a "convenience fee" of a couple bucks.

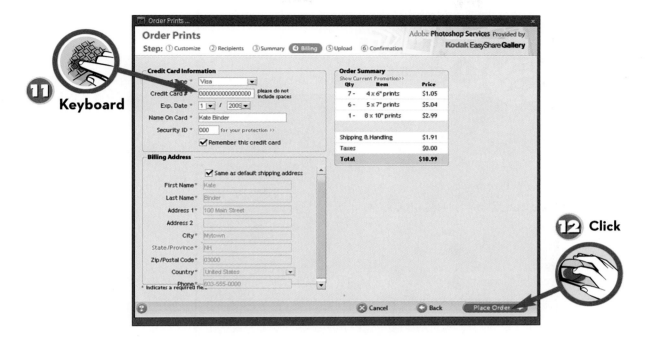

11 Enter your payment information.

12 Click **Place Order**.

End

NOTE
Do It Yourself
You can, of course, print your photos yourself using a desktop inkjet or dye-sublimation photo printer. Check out Part 2, "Getting It All Together," to learn more.

CREATING A PHOTO BOOK

Photo books are the coolest gift ever. It really adds a special air to your photos to see them professionally printed in a real, hardbound book. You can also use the Photo Book Wizard to create a file that you print yourself on your own printer. Either way, Photoshop Elements offers you plenty of templates and page layouts to make your book a truly individual creation.

1 Ctrl-click

Start

2 Click

3 Click

1. In the Organizer, **Ctrl-click** to select the photos you want to include in your book.

2. Click **Create**.

3. Click **Photo Book**.

Continued

NOTE

By the Numbers

The minimum number of pages for a book is 20. However, you can specify a larger number when you choose a theme and layout options, and you can add pages by clicking the Add Page button at the left end of the navigation toolbar.

NOTE

Laying It Out

Let Photoshop Elements choose layouts for each page if you have lots of photos. Otherwise, specify layouts yourself. Photoshop Elements uses lots of multi-photo layouts, so you'll run out of photos before the book is complete.

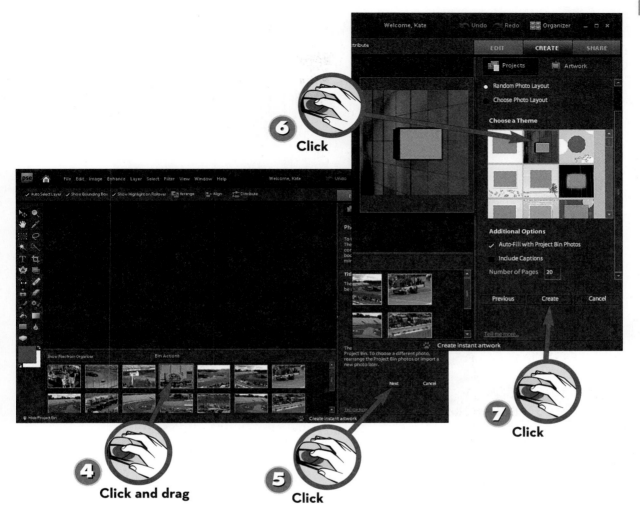

6 **Click**

4 **Click and drag**

5 **Click**

7 **Click**

4 Click and drag photos in the Project Bin to reorder them, placing the title page image in the first slot.

5 Click **Next**.

6 Click a theme.

7 Click **Create**.

Continued

TIP

Control Freak

If you want more control over the layout of your book, click the radio button marked **Choose Photo Layout**, and click off **Auto Fill with Project Bin Photos**. Then you can specify your own layout for each page.

NOTE

Even Fancier

Because Photoshop Elements stores each photo in your book on a separate layer, you can apply layer styles to the pictures. Click the image, and then choose an effect from the Effects palette, then click **Apply**.

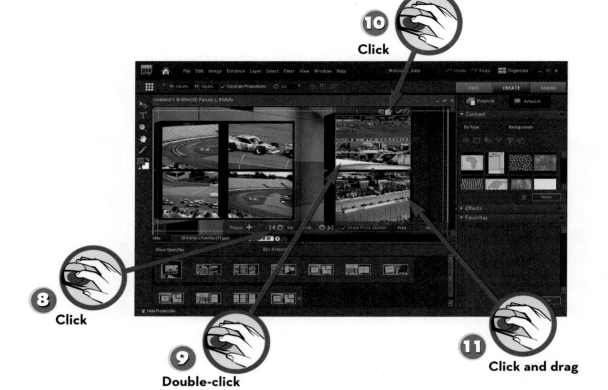

10 Click

8 Click

9 Double-click

11 Click and drag

8 Click the **Next Page** and **Previous Page** buttons to move through the book's pages.

9 To adjust a photo's size or rotation, double-click the photo.

10 After double-clicking the photo, drag the slider to resize or click the button to rotate.

11 After double-clicking a photo, drag and drop the photo onto another photo to swap their positions.

Continued

 TIP
Jazzing It Up
To add a little extra "something" to your book, check out the "clip art" images in the Content palette. Click and drag any picture onto the page to insert it in the book, and then drag a corner handle to resize the image to suit your taste.

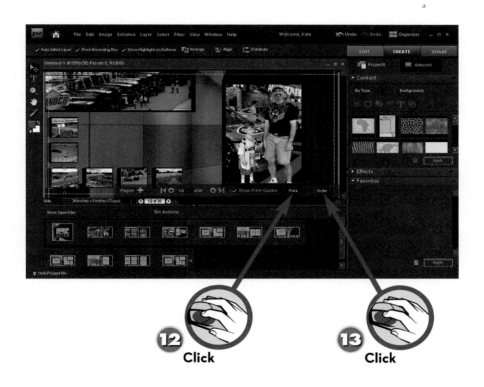

12 Click **Print** to print the book on your own printer.

13 Click **Order** to buy a copy of the book.

End

NOTE

Hey, You! Yeah, You!

If you're the type who clicks right through warning dialogs, you may not have noticed Photoshop Elements warning you that it takes some time to create a file for printing your book. Don't be alarmed when your computer is tied up for a while creating the file; it'll be done soon.

JUST FOR FUN

It's only after you've mastered a set of tools that you can begin to take real joy in using them. Then, you can let the logical, step-by-step calculating part of your brain take a back seat and let your imagination do the driving.

If you've worked through most, if not all, of the preceding tasks, you're ready—and you've earned the right—to have some fun. Tasks in this Part are all about fooling around, experimenting, and exploring ways of manipulating electronic images like collage artists use paper cutouts and a set of paints.

There isn't space in this little book to take you through all the things you can do with Photoshop Elements (if, with so many possible choices and combinations, it's possible in any book). But with the basic skills you've picked up here, your work with this incredibly rich and flexible computer application will start to seem more like play. As you continue to explore, you'll sweat the technical details less and less, and you'll find a marvelous new outlet for your personal expression.

And if, perchance, some of your fantasies seem, er, just a bit bizarre—add a talk bubble or a clever caption and turn them into personalized greeting cards!

BRANCHING OUT

Ever wonder how to turn a simple portrait into a work of art?

Long ago, in a land far away...

PLACING ARTWORK IN AN IMAGE

Commands you might already have used for combining imagery are File, New from Clipboard; File, Import; and the pair Edit, Copy and Edit, Paste. Here's a handy alternative, a quicker way to insert artwork from an external file that's in one of the other Adobe formats (.ai, .eps, .pdf, or .pdp extensions).

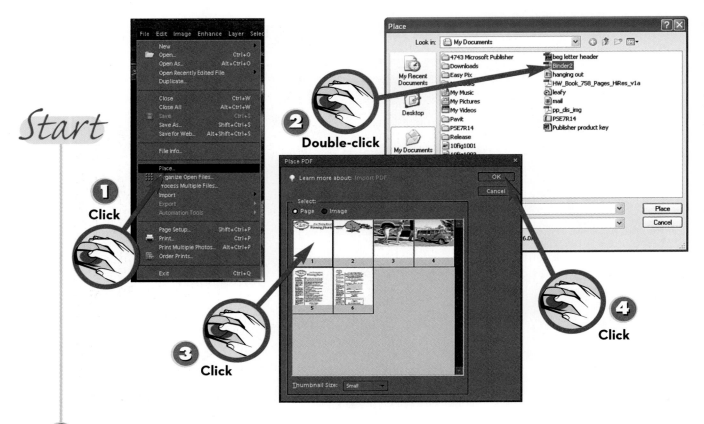

Start

Click ①

Double-click ②

Click ③

Click ④

① With a background image in the active image area, choose **File**, **Place**.

② Locate and double-click the file that contains the artwork (or click it and click **Place**).

③ If the file contains multiple pages, choose the page you want to insert.

④ Click **OK**. The artwork or page is inserted into a new layer in the active image.

Continued

NOTE

Missing Fonts

If you see this warning window after step 3, choose **Continue**, and some other fonts that are available in your computer will be substituted.

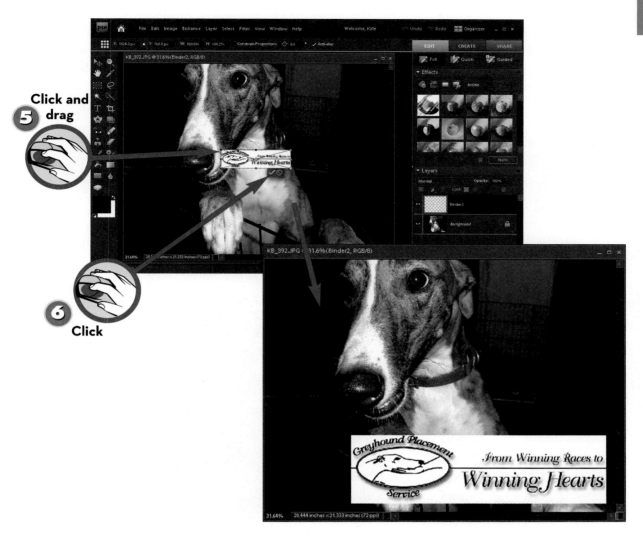

Click and drag 5

6 **Click**

5 Optionally, drag a handle to move or resize the artwork to fit your canvas.

6 Click the **Commit** button, or press **Enter**.

End

 TIP
Vectors Get Rasterized
Vector graphics in the source file get simplified, or *rasterized* (converted to pixels), when you click Commit. The objects take on the same resolution as the target image.

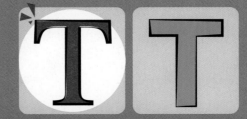

MAKING MOSAIC TILES

Hand-painted tiles are so expensive—and you have to be a real artist to create your own. Unless, that is, you have Photoshop Elements. Here's a quick way to turn any photograph into a pretty convincing tile mosaic.

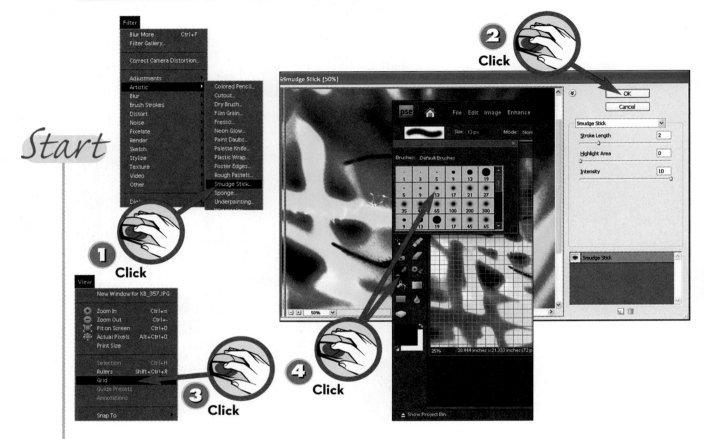

Start

1 With an image open in the Editor's Full Edit mode, choose **Filter**, **Artistic**, **Smudge Stick**.

2 Click **OK**.

3 Choose **View**, **Grid**.

4 Choose the **Brush** tool and pick a small, soft brush.

Continued

TIP

Making It Real

Mount your "tiles" on a tabletop using spray adhesive and a few coats of nonyellowing polyurethane varnish. Or, put your mosaic on a wall—but mount the paper on a thin sheet of wood first, so that you can take it with you when you move.

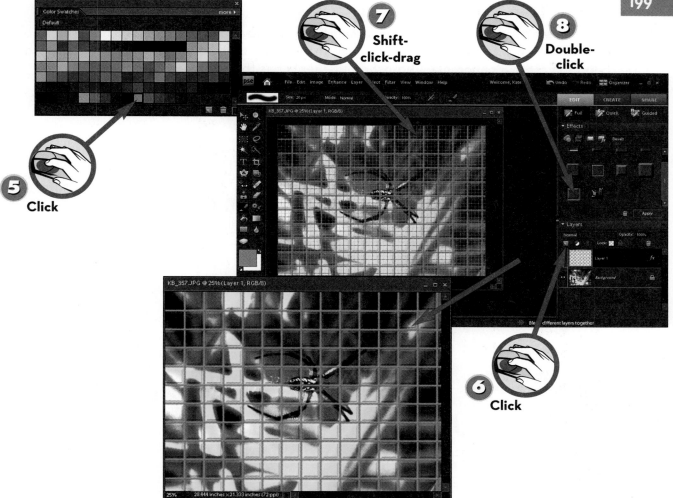

5 In the Color Swatches palette (choose **Window**, **Color Swatches** if it's not visible), choose a foreground color for the grout between the tiles.

6 Click the **Create New Layer** button in the Layers palette, then click **OK**.

7 Hold down **Shift** and click and drag to paint the grout lines along the grid.

8 Double-click the **Simple Sharp Pillow Emboss** style in the Effects palette.

End

NOTE
Get Creative!
Try any filter or combination of filters in step 1—you don't have to use Smudge Stick. You can also adjust the grout width (choose a different brush size).

TIP
Changing Your Mind
To change the grout color, make the grout layer active and choose a new foreground color. Click the **Lock Transparent Pixels** check box at the top of the Layers palette, and then press **Alt+Delete** to replace all the layer's white pixels with the new color.

CREATING PANORAMIC VIEWS

Sometimes, no matter how great your camera is, its viewfinder just can't contain the whole picture. When you want to show an image that's wider than your camera's image area, you need to create a panorama. Photoshop Elements has the smarts to blend the edges of several scenic photos seamlessly into one gorgeous panorama.

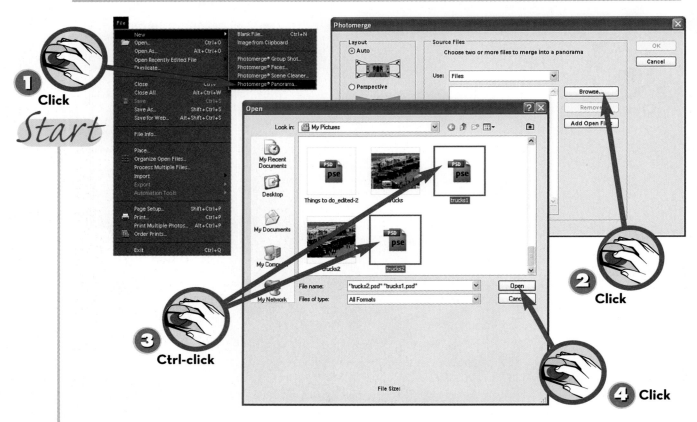

1 With all files closed, choose **File, New Photomerge® Panorama**.

2 Click **Browse**.

3 **Ctrl-click** two or more images to combine.

4 Click **OK**.

Continued

TIP

Pan Your Snaps

Shots must be adjacent so their edges align: Mount the camera on a tripod. Take your source photos all at the same vertical angle, *panning* from left to right, so that the edges overlap the scene.

5 Choose a layout option. (Auto is usually the best choice.)

6 Click **OK**.

End

TIP
Photomerge Options
Perspective can heighten the panoramic effect. **Cylindrical** emphasizes curvature. **Reposition** only doesn't adjust perspective at all, just image rotation and size. Using **Interactive Layout**, you can drag the photos into the correct relative positions yourself.

TIP
Crop to Finish
If you want your image to be rectangular, finish off by cropping it. Even if it's almost rectangular, the horizontal edge of the composite image probably won't be smooth.

TURNING A PHOTO INTO A RUBBER STAMP

Rubber stamps are just plain fun to play with, especially once you get into all the fancy inks, embossing powders, and the like. And with Photoshop Elements, you're not restricted to the stamps you find at the store—you can make your own.

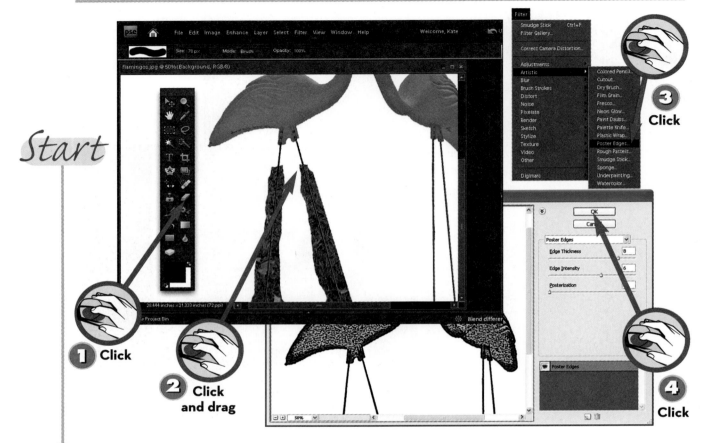

Start

1 **Click**

2 **Click and drag**

3 **Click**

4 **Click**

1 With an image open, choose the **Eraser** tool.

2 Click and drag to erase the image's background, leaving only the portion you want to be the stamp.

3 Choose **Filter**, **Artistic**, **Poster Edges**.

4 Adjust the settings so the areas that will be the stamp are black; then click **OK**.

Continued

TIP
Contrast Is the Key
For the best results, choose a picture of an object against a contrasting background. It helps if there's some contrast within the object's outlines, too, unless it's recognizable merely from its silhouette.

NOTE
From Concept to Reality
When your artwork is ready, convert it into a rubber stamp by using the services of Create a Stamp (www.createastamp.com), The Stampin' Place (www.stampin.com), Simon's Stamps (www.simonstamp.com), or other specialists.

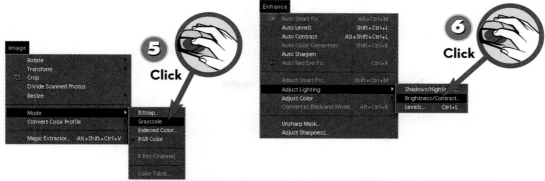

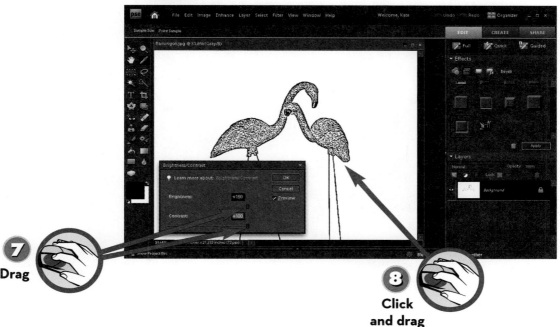

5 Choose **Image**, **Mode**, **Grayscale**, then click **OK**.

6 Choose **Enhance**, **Adjust Lighting**, **Brightness/Contrast**.

7 Drag both sliders all the way to the right and click **OK**.

8 Click and drag the **Eraser** tool to clean up around the stamp's edges if necessary.

End

TIP

Lighten Up

After step 5, if your picture has a lot of dark gray in areas that you want white, choose **Enhance**, **Adjust Lighting**, **Levels**, and drag the middle slider to the left to lighten the midtones so that they'll drop out to white in step 7.

NOTE

What Else It's Good For

This technique is also useful for making coloring pages for the kids, t-shirt artwork, or any kind of art that needs to be black on white.

GETTING AN ANTIQUE LOOK

Of course, "antique" is relative to your age—or the ages of the relatives you want to transform. In this case, decreasing the saturation setting creates a look of old, faded Kodachrome. Adding Film Grain enhances the realism, and the Feather effect on the border adds to the impression of a faded snapshot.

Start

1 With a photo in the active image window, choose **Enhance**, **Adjust Color**, **Adjust Hue/Saturation**.

2 Drag the sliders to decrease the **Saturation** and adjust the **Lightness** as seems appropriate.

3 Click **OK**.

Continued

TIP

Fading and Sepia

Decreasing Saturation can create a monochrome picture, but one that still contains color information. You can then apply Color Variations to get a sepia effect. By contrast, choosing **Image**, **Mode**, **Grayscale** discards all color.

TIP

Remove Color Command

An alternative conversion to grayscale that still preserves color information is the command **Enhance**, **Adjust Color**, **Remove Color**, which makes red, green, and blue values equal and reduces Saturation to zero.

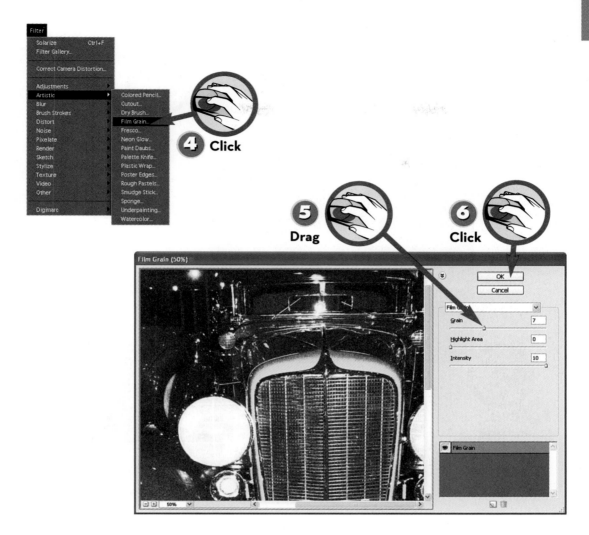

Drag

Click

4 Choose **Filter**, **Artistic**, **Film Grain**.

5 Drag the sliders to adjust the effect, such as increasing the Grain size.

6 Click **OK**.

Continued

TIP

Film Grain

This same type of filter can be applied in the Adobe After Effects application to make your DV movies look like film.

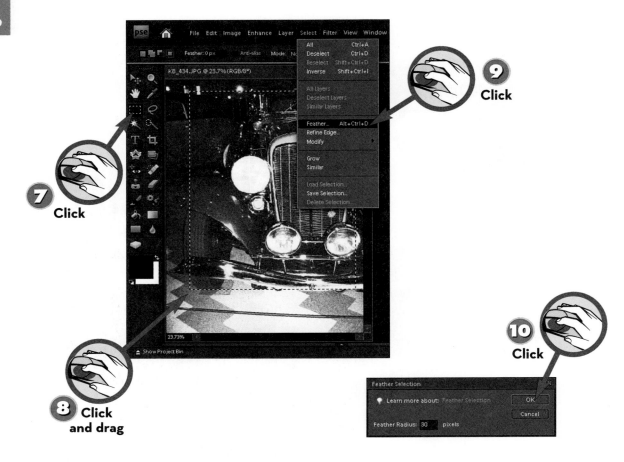

7 Choose the **Rectangular Marquee** tool, or press **M**.

8 Click and drag to size a border around the picture.

9 Choose **Select**, **Feather**.

10 Enter a Feathering value and click **OK**.

Continued

TIP

Feather Radius

In step 10, remember that the size of the Feather effect is proportional to Image Size in pixels. For example, you may have to increase the Radius value to make the effect more obvious.

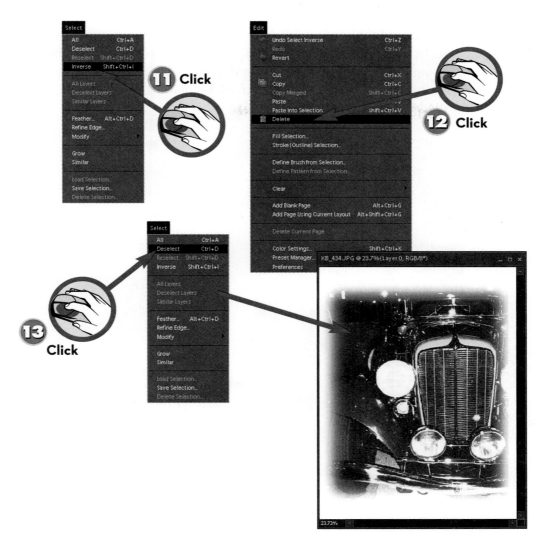

11   Choose **Select**, **Inverse**, or press **Shift+Ctrl+I**.

12   Choose **Edit**, **Delete**.

13   Choose **Select**, **Deselect**, or press **Ctrl+D**.

End

TIP
Experiment!
This kind of experimentation with Photoshop Elements
can bring into play any and all the techniques you've
learned in this book. Have fun!

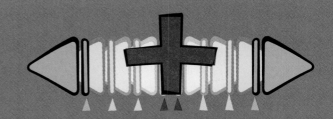

CREATING POP ART

The biggest advantage of digital photo editing is that you can try dozens, hundreds, or even thousands of variations on a theme for each photo. And putting a few variations together in a collage format just happens to be a recognized art technique, one made famous by none other than Andy Warhol. Give it a try!

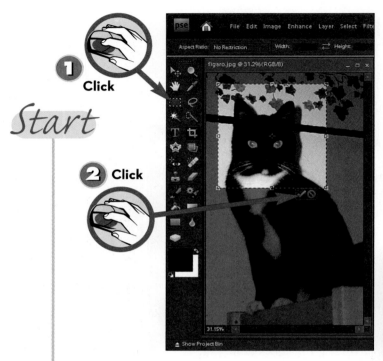

Start

1 Click

2 Click

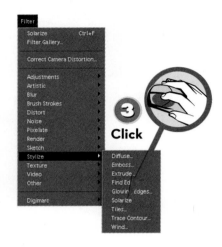

3 Click

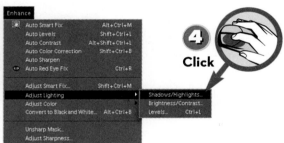

4 Click

1 With an image open in the Editor's Full Edit mode, switch to the **Crop** tool and **Shift-drag** in the image to draw a square cropping marquee.

2 Click the **Commit** button below the cropping marquee.

3 Choose **Filter**, **Stylize**, **Solarize**.

4 Choose **Enhance**, **Adjust Lighting**, **Shadows/Highlights**.

Continued

TIP

More Options

You don't have to be restricted to different color schemes for your variations. Try applying different Artistic filters. Or line up several copies of an image in a row and make each copy a bit lighter or a bit darker than the one next to it.

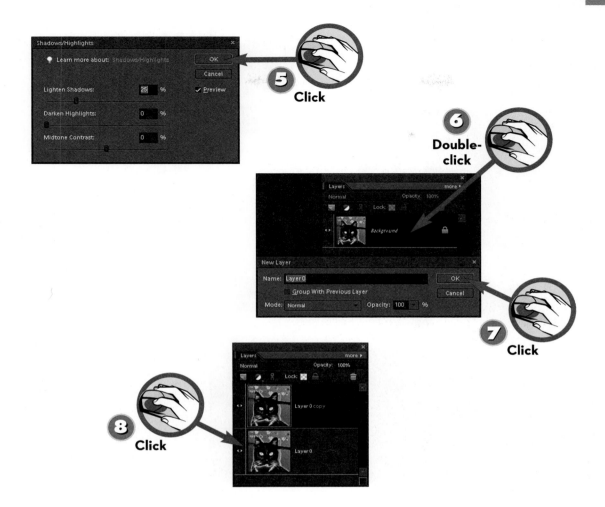

5. Click **OK**.

6. In the Layers palette, double-click the **Background**.

7. Click **OK**.

8. Drag Layer 0 onto the **Create Layer** button to duplicate it.

Continued

 NOTE
Separation of Layers
Putting each copy of the image on its own layer makes moving it around and applying color changes to it easy.

 TIP
Test Run
Make sure the picture you use has strong enough lines that you'll still be able to tell what it is after you run the Solarize filter. If you're not sure, test it by choosing **Filter**, **Stylize**, **Solarize** before you spend any time cropping it.

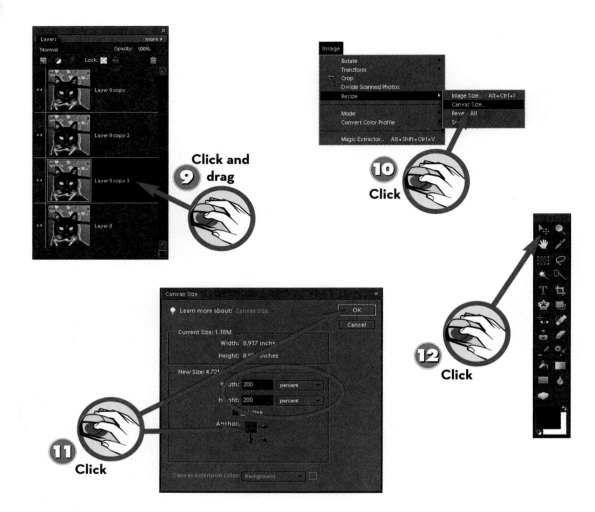

Click and drag 9

Click 10

Click 12

Click 11

9 Repeat step 8 twice to create a total of four layers in the image.

10 Choose **Image**, **Resize**, **Canvas Size**.

11 Click the upper-left corner of the proxy grid and set the **Width** and **Height** to 200%; then click **OK**.

12 Choose the **Move** tool.

 Continued

TIP
A Prerequisite
To select each layer with the Move tool, Auto Select Layer must be checked in the options bar.

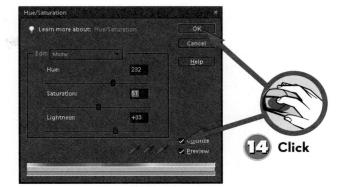

13 Click

14 Click

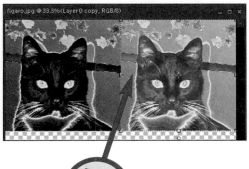

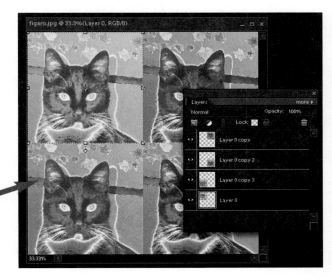

15 Shift-drag

16 Shift-drag

13 Click in the upper-left corner of the image and choose **Enhance, Adjust Color, Adjust Hue/Saturation**.

14 Click **Colorize** and drag the sliders until you like the image's color; then click **OK**.

15 Shift-drag the picture to the right side of the window.

16 Repeat steps 13–15 to move the other picture duplicates to the bottom corners of the window and colorize them with different colors.

End

NOTE
Enlarging Your Color Palette
In step 14, you can adjust the Saturation and Lightness sliders. Leaving these settings the same for all four images provides a more consistent look, but varying them enables you to use a wider range of colors and tints.

TIP
Lining Things Up
Press **Shift** as you drag the layers to constrain their movement to 45° angles: straight up and down, left and right, or corner to corner.

A

active image area   Application window that displays the image contained in the currently open file.

active layer   Virtual drawing plane currently selected in an open image.

adjustment layer   In a multilayered image, a layer containing no pixels, inserted to affect the overall appearance of all layers beneath it; in effect, a digital photographic filter.

autofocus   Automatic focusing capability of digital cameras.

automatic white balance   Digital camera function that reproduces colors based on the assumption that the lightest area in the frame is pure white.

autoselect   Procedure whereby selecting a shape or text object with the Move tool automatically causes its layer to be selected, too.

B

backlight   Photographic light source emanating from behind the subject.

base layer   When layers are grouped, the bottommost layer that sets the boundaries of the upper ones, determined by the boundaries of a shape on that layer.

bitmap   Digital image composed of pixels; raster image; pixel array; in Photoshop Elements color modes, a black-and-white image.

Blending mode   In a multilayered image, a layer option that determines how colors on different layers combine; an option for various tools and filters. Examples: Normal, Dissolve, Hard, Soft.

blow out   To totally overexpose an area of an image so that it is pure white and contains no picture detail.

brush dynamics   Options for the size, shape, and behavior of the Brush tool that control the quality of its brush stroke.

brush tip   Size and shape of the tip of the Brush tool, set in the Options bar after the tool is selected.

burn   A traditional darkroom technique by which you underexpose masked areas of a film negative before making a print.

C

canvas size   Paper or media size associated with an image file.

caption   Printable text that describes the content of a picture.

capture   To upload image data from a camera, camcorder, or scanner into a computer.

catalog   In Organizer, a collection of image files from which a presentation can be created.

Clipboard   Scratchpad memory area in the system software through which data, including graphics and images, can be exchanged between open applications.

Close box   X button in the top-right corner of any Windows window by which it may be closed, or turned off.

CMYK   Color model and mixing scheme used in Photoshop but not in Photoshop Elements. Based on the components cyan, magenta, yellow, and black. Inkjet printers and printing presses use inks in these four colors to print.

collage   Art term for a composition made from cut-out images pasted onto a board.

color cast   Overall tint of a photograph, particularly noticeable and in need of correction when it creates unflattering flesh tones in the subjects.

color components   Separate channels, or primary colors, within a color model; red, green, and blue in the RGB color model; hue, saturation, and lightness in the HSL model.

color management   Coordination of color devices, such as cameras, computer screens, and printers, so that colors rendered on all of them appear to match.

color matching   Fine-tuning the output of two or more color-reproduction devices, such as a monitor and a printer, so that colors appear the same on both.

color space   The range of all colors available in a color model.

composite   Combination or merging two or more images.

composition   Artistic arrangement of subjects within the picture area.

compression   Mathematical transformation of a digital file so as to describe its contents using less data, thereby creating a smaller file, while degrading its quality or accuracy as little as possible.

constrain   To limit the repositioning or resizing of a shape or text to perpendicular angles; to prevent distortion; to maintain proportions (aspect ratio).

contact sheet   Film photographer's reference print created in the darkroom by exposing filmstrips in direct contact with a sheet of print paper.

contrast   Range of brightness between the highlights and shadows in a photograph.

crop   To reframe an image, moving its edges to exclude unwanted areas.

crushed blacks   Underexposed areas of a picture that are totally black and contain no picture detail.

D

default   Preselected program option settings.

digital watermark   Invisible copyright or proprietary notice within the image area of a photograph that can be read by Photoshop Elements or special reader software.

digitize　To convert a film print or analog video clip to a digital file; to scan a photo.

discard layers　To merge and simplify all layers in an image simultaneously, rendering text and artwork uneditable as objects; see also *flatten*.

dither　To render a subtle color by juxtaposing dots of two or more primary colors.

dodge　In traditional darkroom technique, to overexpose unmasked areas of a film negative before making a print.

dpi　Unit of resolution of a digital printer; dots per inch; equivalent to pixels/inch.

duotone　Two-color image.

DV　Abbreviation of the Digital Video recording standard.

DVD　Abbreviation for Digital Versatile Disc; optical recording medium for videos and movies.

DVD menu　Onscreen selections of DVD chapters, each indicated by a button.

E

exposure　Length of time light is permitted to strike a camera's film or sensors (called *CCD chips* in a digital camera).

extension　In a computer filename, characters to the right of the rightmost period, indicating the file format (for example, .psd, .jpg, .doc, .mpeg).

eyelight　Small photographic light source aimed directly into a subject's eyes to make the eyes sparkle.

F

feather　Blurred edges of a shape; vignette.

file format　Indicated by the extension in the filename, the type of file (such as a native Photoshop file).

fill　Solid area or pattern within a shape, text, or image area.

fill flash　Bright photographic light source used to supplement key light and fill in the area surrounding the subject. In Photoshop Elements, the ability to lighten the darkest (usually foreground) areas of a photo, leaving the bright (usually background) areas unchanged.

filter　In Photoshop Elements, a pre-built artistic effect that can be applied to an image; in conventional photography, a glass covering for a lens that changes the quality of light.

FireWire　Apple trademark for the connection between a camcorder or other device and a computer, designated IEEE 1394; equivalent to Sony's i.LINK.

flatten　To merge and simplify all layers in an image simultaneously; see also *discard layers*.

flip　To create a mirror image of a shape, text, or image.

focus   In Photoshop Elements, to sharpen or blur the edges of a selection; in conventional photography, to adjust the camera lens to achieve the same effect.

folder   In a computer file system, a named directory that contains files.

font   In typography, a typeface in a particular point size; in computer applications, a typeface.

f-stop   Camera setting that controls how much light is admitted during an exposure.

FTP   Abbreviation of File Transfer Protocol, a method of uploading files to the Internet.

Full Edit mode   Interface view that enables access to all features of Photoshop Elements. See also *Guided Edit mode* and *Quick Fix mode*.

G

Gaussian blur   Named for mathematician Carl Friedrich Gauss, a filter that enables finer control over how an image is blurred than does Blur or Blur More.

gradient   Blended color used to fill a shape or background.

grain   Noise filter applied to a digital image to simulate the grain of photographic film.

grayed out   Dimmed; refers to menu commands or dialog box options that are unavailable based on current settings.

grayscale   Monochrome picture that contains shades of black and white.

group   Combination of palettes or layers so that they can be manipulated as a single palette or object.

Guided Edit mode   Interface view that provides instructions for completing common tasks and restricts access to commands and tools other than those needed for the task at hand. See also *Full Edit mode* and *Quick Fix mode*.

H

halation effect   Artifact of early film that created a beatific glow around close-ups of movie stars.

halftone screen   Dot pattern used in commercial printing to render shaded images using tiny, solid dots of black (B&W) or four primary colors (CMYK).

handle   Corner on a selection that can be dragged to resize or reposition the object.

hard   Quality of light that produces sharp edges and dark shadows.

hidden tool   Any tool in the toolbar that can be selected by right-clicking a related tool.

HSL   Color model and mixing scheme based on components hue (primary color), saturation (tint), and lightness (light-dark value).

I

ICC   Abbreviation of International Color Consortium, which promotes color standards for the printing industry.

Impressionist brush   Tool used to lay down blurred brush strokes, after the technique of painters who rebelled against doing pictures in painstaking detail.

indexed color   Restricted color tables for specific uses, such as Web or Windows system display.

ink-and-paint   Conventional movie animator's technique of drawing a cartoon character's outline in ink on a clear sheet of celluloid and then filling in solid shapes with acrylic paint.

intellectual property rights (IPR) Copyrights, patents, and trademarks; copyright applies to photographs, to which the photographer is author and rights holder.

K

key light   Main photographic light source aimed to highlight the subject.

keystoning   Photographic distortion produced by aiming the camera at a steep angle, high or low, in relation to the subject.

L

landscape   Rectangular image or printer orientation with the long dimension horizontal.

layer   Separate drawing, painting, text, or image plane among multiple planes, or layers, in a Photoshop image.

layer style   Options, such as bevels or drop shadows, that affect all objects on a given layer.

level   Value of red, green, blue, or black input or output channel to produce brightness and contrast.

linking layers   Marking and associating layers so that they can be manipulated together.

lossless   File compression that results in no perceptible loss of quality or accuracy.

lossy   File compression that *does* result in a loss of quality or accuracy.

LZW   File compression scheme based on a transformation named for mathematicians Lempel, Ziv, and Welch.

M

mapping   Transformation that bends and spreads an image or texture over the surface of an object.

mask   To cover part of an image so that the area is unaffected by changes made to other areas of the image.

menu bar   Main pull-down program commands in an application such as Photoshop Elements, near the top of the program window, beginning with the File menu on the left and proceeding to the Help menu on the right.

merge   To both simplify and combine layers in a single operation.

midtone   Pixel values in the middle range between highlights and shadows.

mixed media   Art term for works that may combine assemblage, collage, and painting or drawing.

mode   Image rendering as either grayscale or color.

monochrome   Single-color image, but not necessarily black and white.

multisession   Describing a CD or DVD to which files can be written, or appended, at different times.

N–O

navigate   Procedure for finding files and folders by exploring the file system, based on a hierarchy of files within folders (possibly within other folders) on a storage device (such as a disk).

negative   Reverse image from processing camera film, resulting in shadow areas rendered as highlights, highlights as shadows, and color primaries as their opposites (red as cyan, blue as yellow, and so on).

nudge   To move a selection by small increments by pressing the arrow keys.

opacity   Degree to which light is blocked by an object or layer; inverse of transparency.

Options bar   Settings for a tool, such as Brush, that become available beneath the menu bar after the tool has been selected.

Organizer   Photoshop Elements component that catalogs photos and provides access to printing and online display methods.

orientation   Rotation angle of an image or printout; portrait or landscape.

P

palette   Floating window containing effects, commands, and help grouped by category.

Palette Bin   Storage location in the work area for frequently used palettes.

palette tab   Handle by which a palette can be selected, docked, or undocked from the Palette Bin.

pan   To rotate a camera, typically mounted on a tripod, from left to right or from right to left in the same horizontal plane.

panorama   Scenic, wide-angle landscape; Photomerge output.

picture package   Assortment of prints in various sizes, from wallet-sized to larger sizes suitable for framing, offered by commercial photographers.

pixel   Picture element; colored dot in a bitmap image.

pixels/inch   Resolution of a raster image; equivalent to printer dots per inch (dpi).

place   To insert artwork from an external file into an open image.

plug-in   Add-on software module that extends the capability of an application.

point size   Size of type in a selected font.

Pointillize filter   Limiting brush strokes to tiny dots of primary color; technique pioneered by Impressionist painter Georges Seurat.

port   Input/output connector on a computer.

portrait   Rectangular image or printer orientation with the long dimension vertical; headshot.

posterization   Garish color effect produced by the command Image, Adjustments, Posterize.

preferences   User option settings that override default values.

printable area   Rectangular area of a printout that excludes margins where the printer grips the paper, and therefore where it can't print an image.

profile   Stored color table used for color management.

Progressive mode   JPEG file setting that causes a downloaded image to be built up in visible stages, intended to improve the viewing experience over slow connections.

publish   To upload files to the World Wide Web.

Q

Quick Fix mode   Interface view that simplifies and streamlines features of Photoshop Elements so that corrections can be applied more easily, but with limited user control. See also *Full Edit mode* and *Guided Edit mode*.

R

rasterize   To convert a vector shape or type object to pixels; to simplify.

recipe   Sequential instructions delivered by the Help system for performing a specific task.

red eye   Undesirable reflection in a subject's eyes caused by flash photography.

redo   Reverse the preceding Undo command.

related topics   Help selections that appear in the Hints palette after doing a search.

render   To apply changes to a digital image and display or print it.

resample   To change the resolution (pixels/inch) of an image.

reset   To return to previous option settings.

resolution   Measure of picture quality or degree of detail; pixels/inch; dpi.

retouch To use artistic techniques to improve the appearance of photographic subjects or scenes; in portrait work, to soften wrinkles, remove blemishes, and so on.

revert To cancel pending edits without saving and return to the original version of a file; see also *undo*.

RGB Color model and mixing scheme used in Photoshop Elements, based on components red, green, and blue.

S

search field Text box in the top-right center of the Photoshop Elements work area into which a text description of a problem or task can be typed in order to search the Help files.

selection Active object or area within the image area to which the next command or operation will be applied.

sepia Brown-tinted monochrome image; typical of antique photographs.

shape Geometric object in Photoshop Elements (for example, rectangle, ellipse).

sharpen To increase pixel contrast at object boundaries; to bring into focus.

shortcuts bar Row of buttons with icons just beneath the menu bar, representing single-click activation of commonly used commands.

simplify To convert a vector shape or type to pixels; to rasterize.

skew To apply a spatial transformation to a selected object that causes its sides to be slanted.

slider Program control in some dialog boxes, toolbars, and palettes that can be adjusted by clicking and dragging.

Smart Paint Special effects that can be applied with a brush and modified or removed after they are applied.

soft Blurred; out of focus.

stacking order Priority of layers in a multilayered image that determines visibility of objects; objects on upper layers will obscure overlapping objects beneath.

still Single-frame photographic image (as opposed to a moving image created by a sequence of frames in a movie or video).

streaming video Video clip, usually low resolution, optimized for downloading over the Web.

superimpose To overlay one graphic object on another.

swatch A single, saved color; one of a table of color selections coordinated for a specific purpose, such as Web-safe colors.

system colors Set of swatches containing only colors displayable without dithering on Windows computers.

T

texture   Variegated surface or area; pattern.

thumbnail   Small, low-resolution image used to preview file selections without having to spend time opening the full-resolution file.

title bar   Top band on any Windows window showing the name of its selections (or filename of the image or document it contains), and by which the window may be moved by clicking and dragging.

tool   One of the selection, drawing, and retouching tools found in the Photoshop Elements toolbar, located by default at the left edge of the work area.

toolbox   Collection of Photoshop Elements tools, located by default at the left edge of the work area.

ToolTip   Name or function of a tool or button, as well as its shortcut key (if any), which pops up when you hover the pointer over it before making a selection.

transparency   Degree to which objects and colors on underlying layers are visible; the inverse of opacity.

tutorial   Online training lesson available through the Help menu.

type mask   Type-shaped selection area, typically used to create hollow text to let the background or a lower layer show through.

U–V

undo   To reverse or cancel the most recently executed command or change; see also *redo*.

undock   To open a palette from the Palette Bin.

ungroup   To make a previously grouped set of palettes or layers accessible individually; see also *group*.

upload   To transfer a digital file from a device, such as a camera, camcorder, or scanner, to a computer; to capture.

USB   Abbreviation for Universal Serial Bus; a type of computer port that supports digital cameras and printers.

vector   Mathematical description of a geometric object; a resolution-independent object description.

vignette   Portrait with feathered edges.

W–Z

Website index page   Home page on the World Wide Web.

WIA   Abbreviation of Windows Image Acquisition, a standard for connecting scanners and cameras to computers.

ZIP   Lossless file compression scheme.

zoom   To magnify the view of an image.

Index

D

S

Index

T

U-V

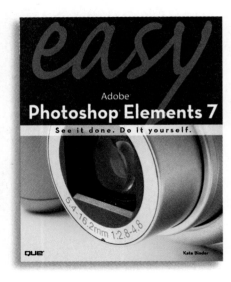

FREE Online Edition

Your purchase of **Easy Adobe® Photoshop® Elements 7** includes access to a free online edition for 45 days through the Safari Books Online subscription service. Nearly every Que book is available online through Safari Books Online, along with more than 5,000 other technical books and videos from publishers such as Addison-Wesley Professional, Cisco Press, Exam Cram, IBM Press, O'Reilly, Prentice Hall, and Sams.

SAFARI BOOKS ONLINE allows you to search for a specific answer, cut and paste code, download chapters, and stay current with emerging technologies.

Activate your FREE Online Edition at www.informit.com/safarifree

> **STEP 1:** Enter the coupon code: UTCVJGA.

> **STEP 2:** New Safari users, complete the brief registration form. Safari subscribers, just log in.

If you have difficulty registering on Safari or accessing the online edition, please e-mail customer-service@safaribooksonline.com

JUN 16 '09